Publisher & Writer's

CYCLODEPIC DICTIONARY

Gerald L. Shingleton

CONTENTS

NOTE

Writing and publishing is a vast subject, so immense in fact that including every up-to-date term would be next to impossible. Every day, it would seem, something new is introduced to the industry. So starting with rudimentary items and expanding in future editions would be the most ideal approach in this endeavor. Terms are alphabetized. Ideally, a new author or publisher is advised to leisurely read the book's entire contents to familiarize themselves with industry expressions. Of course, times amend things; companies go out of business or change names, websites close, and some terms become obsolete while new ones are created. So, in this first edition, only industry essential words and expressions have been included with the idea that there's more to come, especially in an ever-changing field.

The reason this reference is valuable is simply because anyone unfamiliar with the business wouldn't even know a key element to look up. Additional information regarding all subject matter (including current pricing, active hyperlinks, and trends) is of course, available on the internet and recommended for full comprehensive knowledge.

There are no terms, definitions, advice, or guidance regarding the actual business aspects of publishing including Title Profits, loss statements, goal setting topics, budgeting, cash flow analysis, income reports, balance sheets, planning, contracts, distribution legalities, operations, book channels, checklists, marketing plans, author questionnaires, subsidiary rights forms, or book club templates. Topics such as these are left for text books and professors.

DICTIONARY LISTING LEGEND

◊**SYMBOL**   The identification mark preceding the word stands for an Amazon.com related term.

▪**SYMBOL**   The identification mark preceding the word stands for an industry generic term.

○**SYMBOL**   The identification mark preceding the word stands for an industry related company or commercial term.

1 A-A

A

◇A9

A9 was created by Amazon.com in 2003. There's a significance to the letter and number in this term. The letter "**A**" has sort of a duality meaning. It could stand for "Amazon", but it really doesn't. The only purpose of A9.com was to leverage complex step by step calculations, and the name was chosen as a clever number based word representing ALGORITHMS (i.e. 'A' + 9 other letters).

A9 is an independent company aimed at producing technology advances in Search and Advertising. A9 focuses on several areas like Product, Cloud, Visual, and a Search Advertising platform technology. Some early A9 services such as "Search Inside the Book" continue today, while others have been discontinued.

▪AA

AA is the abbreviation for Author's Alterations. The symbol is in contrast to PE which means printer's error. AA are changes occurring during the typesetting or printing process and usually an extra service charged to the author.

○ **AAP**

AAP stands for the Association of American Publishers. There are more than 200,000 members in over three hundred companies. They span all categories of publishing and represent the major commercial, educational and professional companies as well as independents, non-profits, university presses and scholarly societies. AAP is the trade association for the U.S. book publishers, providing advocacy and communications on behalf of the industry.

○ **AAUP**

AAUP stands for the Association of American University Presses. Formally established in 1937, AAUP promotes and influences the work of university presses, provides shared marketing opportunities, and helps its 130+ member organizations fulfill common commitments to scholarships and society. AAUP members participate in several scholarly disciplines, including the humanities, the arts, and sciences, and are innovators in the world of electronic publishing.

○ **ABA**

ABA stands for the American Booksellers Association, a trade association of booksellers; a non-profit trade association founded in 1900 that promotes independent bookstores in the United States and Canada. Members actively support freedom of speech through their Foundation for Free Expression, literacy, and other programs that encourage reading. Independent booksellers openly express concern about potential negative impacts on free speech by giant nationwide web retailers. They feel that publishers cater to these retailers who exercise control over what books and ideas are available. That soft censorship will ultimately rest in the hands of these few companies

◊AbeBooks

This Amazon Trademark Company was formed when acquiring twelve year old Canadian company ABEbooks (formerly the Advanced Book Exchange). AbeBooks is an online marketplace for books focusing on used, rare and out of print titles for sale by independent booksellers. It currently has 110 million books for sale from 13,500 sellers. The company has been around since 1996 and fills a niche for Amazon in hard-to-find or out-of-print books. Rather than hold its own inventory, it acts as a digital marketplace for established booksellers. AbeBooks' headquarters remains in Victoria, BC, Canada, and Amazon's European offices will remain in Dusseldorf, Germany. The company continues to support both international and domestic marketplaces in Canada.

▪ABI

ABI is the abbreviation for Advanced Book Information. Publishers supply information concerning their title to *Bowker* for inclusion in *Forthcoming Books* and *Books in Print*. This information is also cross referenced in other databases. An ABI form is filed by the publisher to list books in *Bowker's* directories, such as *Books in Print*.

◊ABNA

Amazon Platform: ABNA stands for Amazon Breakthrough Novel

Award. In 2014, the Manuscript word count was changed to a maximum of 125,000 words for 10,000 eligible entries. For rules and full details on the Contest, visit www.amazon.com/abna. Each First Prize and Grand Prize winner receives a publishing contract with Amazon Publishing, including a $15,000 advance for four First Prize winners and a $50,000 advance for the Grand Prize winner. Learn more about the contest by reading the official rules, and joining the ABNA discussion boards.

■ACCII text file

ACCII stands for American Standard Code for Information Interchange. It is the worldwide standard format for text files in computers and in the Internet. The term (text-file) replaces an old alternative name of "flat-file" which is a type of process categorizer that's a structured program involving a sequence of lines of electronic text. Codes also exists within this systemized computer file system. The end of a text file, for example, is often denoted by placing one or more special characters, known as an end-of-file marker, after the last line. In essence, "Text-file" refers to a type of container, while plain-text refers to a type of content. Text-files can contain plain-text, but they are not limited to such. In other words, for a generic level description, basically there are two kinds of computer files: text-files and binary-files.

■Acquisition Editors

A publisher has an editorial staff. The people who sort through submissions and network with literary agents to find the books the company will publish, are labeled acquisition editors. Their specific duties are to negotiate advances and navigate the book through the entire publishing process.

◊ACX

Audiobook Creation Exchange (**ACX**) makes it easy to find a narrator, produce and distribute an audiobook, and earn royalties. The Amazon Platform is a simple process to turn a book into an audiobook, creating a new revenue stream. ACX connects authors with professional audio producers to create audiobooks. ACX's distribution options and royalties are through online retailers such as iTunes, Amazon, and Audible.

▪**Advance**

A publisher's election to provide an upfront payment against royalties is referred to in the industry as an advance. This is technically a pre-payment for a portion of the expected royalties the author will earn. The amount is determined by the publisher and based on the book's predictable sales for six months.

▪**Advance Reading Copy**

Description: A publisher's preliminary bound book version for author's review and promotional purposes. Sometimes it is issued without the final corrections.

◊**Advantage**

Amazon.com Advantage program is a self-service gateway allowing publishers to set up an *Advantage* account on-line. Once active, they start adding books they intend to source to Amazon. Adding account items automatically reveals which are available from them. To list on-line, an applicant needs a valid legal title to distribute. Once books are enrolled (listed) in the account, Amazon.com will automatically begin ordering them. This typically occurs once a week. The goal is to have the publisher send enough copies to meet current customer demand, along with enough extra to meet that demand for the next few weeks. Instructions are simply to confirm the orders in the Advantage account, and deliver notification when anticipating arrival at an Amazon.com warehouse. Information on shipping rules and guidelines can be found in the online Help Center of the person's Advantage account. Once Amazon.com receives the inventory, it will be stored in one of their world-class fulfillment centers, and be available for purchase. The item will appear as "In-stock" on its Amazon.com product page, where it becomes eligible for Prime(TM) and FREE Super Saver Shipping.

Amazon's self-service consignment program enables publishers to promote and sell books and media products directly on Amazon.com. *Advantage* is designed specifically for publishers, music labels, studios, authors, and other content owners who would like to source their products to Amazon.com. The Advantage program is not intended for individuals selling used copies, or resellers of books (such as bookstores). If that is of particular interest, the applicant should review the other selling options, such as Selling on Amazon and Fulfillment by Amazon.

◊Affiliate

Amazon.com was one of the first online retailers to establish a successful affiliate program, which is a type of performance-based marketing. Using this platform, an affiliate can post a banner advertisement or direct link to an Amazon.com product on their website. If a reader clicks a link and purchases a product from Amazon, the affiliate receives 4 percent to 15 percent of the sale price as a commission, depending on the type of product and other factors. As of the time of publication, Amazon.com continues to operate an affiliate program.

(http://www.ehow.com/info_8672033_amazoncom.html#ixzz2zAuxpfs7)

■Affiliate Marketing

Performance based marketing relies purely on financial motivations to drive sales. In the world of affiliate marketing, there are four core participants; the bookstore and an additional relationship between three parties.

1. **advertiser** can be a company selling a product like electronics, airline tickets, clothing or car parts, or an advertiser could also be an insurance company selling policies. The most important thing to remember is that you are an advertiser if you are ready to pay other people to help you sell and promote your business.

2. **publisher** is an individual or company that promotes an advertiser's product or service in exchange for earning a commission. Advertisers contractually agree to work with a publisher, then provide the publisher with creative – in the form of links, banner or text ads or even unique phone numbers – that the publisher incorporates into their website.

3. **Consumer:** The final component that completes the affiliate relationship triangle is the consumer. The consumer is the one who actually sees the ad and then makes an action (either by clicking a link or by submitting their information via a form) that takes them from the publisher's website to the advertiser's to complete the action, which we call a conversion.

○ AID (ad ID)

AID is a number used by the *affiliate* driven company, Commission Junction. The identification identifies a specific link and enables **CJ** to track creative performance as well as credit the publisher when they earn a commissionable transaction. Because each link has a unique AID, it also allows **CJ** to identify the appropriate advertiser.

◊ Alexa

Alexa is a web based Information Company designed to optimize a posted site and get more traffic. Currently a California-based subsidiary company of Amazon.com, Alexa has the ultimate capacity to provide commercial web traffic data. Originally founded as an independent company in 1996, Alexa was purchased in 1999. The major functionality is basically to collect information based on browsing behavior that in turn transmits data to the website, where it is stored and analyzed, while formulating the basis for web traffic reporting. As of 2014, Alexa provides traffic data, global rankings and other information on 30 million websites, and visited by over 8.8 million people monthly.

http://www.alexa.com/

Analytical insights benchmark, compare and optimize businesses on the web allowing thousands of professionals to access actionable, in-depth acumens. Three plans are available; Basic – Insight – Advanced. Viable Intelligence categories include Historical Traffic Trends, Demographics, Sites Linking In & Upstream Sites, Social Metrics, Engagement, Traffic Sources, Downstream Sites, Organic & Paid Keyword Insights.

○ Alfred A. Knopf

Alfred A. Knopf, or Knopf Publishing Group is a subsidiary of Random House, founded in 1915, that has long been known as a publisher of distinguished hardcover fiction and nonfiction. Its list of authors includes Toni Morrison, John Updike, Cormac McCarthy, Alice Munro, Anne Rice, Anne Tyler, Jane Smiley, Richard Ford, Julia Child, Peter Carey, Kazuo Ishiguro, and Michael Ondaatje, as well as such classic writers as Thomas Mann, Willa Cather, John Hersey, and John Cheever.

○ Alltop

Alltop.com is a valuable website for writers. It is different than a standard search engine in that it answers current global questions based on a huge collection of RSS feeds; headlines and latest stories on file. A free App for the iPad is available.

○ ALA

ALA is the abbreviation for American Library Association. It is the largest and oldest library association in the world. Founded in 1876, the ALA provides industry leadership developing, promoting, and improving library information services.

◊ Amapedia

Amapedia was a wikipedia-inspired product website run by the retailer Amazon.com, that existed from January 2007 to June 2010, where users could edit articles about Amazon's products. At that time, anyone with an account on Amazon.com could edit the contents of Amapedia.com.

◊**Amazon Cart**

#AmazonCart makes it easy for followers to shop directly from Twitter. Now when you tweet an Amazon.com product link with Store ID, Twitter users, who have connected their accounts to Amazon, can add the item directly to their Carts by replying to a tweet with '#AmazonCart'. Any purchase that occurs as a result of a Cart ad via #AmazonCart will be attributed to a Store ID and therefore eligible to earn advertising fees.

◊**AmazonCrossing**

AmazonCrossing is an imprint that publishes foreign book translations from around the world. To learn more about the AmazonCrossing program, visit the program page at

http://www.amazon.com/amazoncrossing.

◊**AmazonEncore**

AmazonEncore is an Amazon imprint that acquires self-published books that have sold well.

◊**Amazon Local Support**

Description: Local deals and services offered by Amazon.com which includes numerous subjects like Vouchers, business growth, account management, and support services. One recent convenience is the ability to download the free Amazon Local app on an Apple or Android Device for All Deals, including restaurants, Bars & Pubs, Entertainment & Travel, Shopping & Services, and Health & Beauty. Customers can improve their Amazon Local experience by setting up the category and location preferences.

Note: There is a customer service hot line for customer service that is not widely publicized. In Canada and U.S., the number is 1-866-216-1072. Spanish Support is 866-749-7538.

◊Amazon Payments

All Amazon.com customers pay for purchases using Amazon Payments. The company doesn't allow phone orders or even permit customers to send checks or money orders. A third-party payment service like PayPal is also not allowed. Everything is electronically programmed where customers are registered with authorized credit card numbers and shipping addresses. Registered sellers automatically receive payments via electronic bank transfers.

◊Amazon Prime

Amazon.com has this membership program that, for an annual fee, provides free two-day shipping for all qualified purchases as well as inexpensive one-day rates and access to free streaming of a variety of Instant Videos.

◊Amazon Publishing

Amazon Trademark; the website is https://www.apub.com. The Publishing arm of Amazon is full-service. With a mission to invent new and better ways to connect authors and readers, Amazon continues to grow and publish in print, e-book, audio, and deluxe formats, as well as Kindle Serials and Kindle Singles. From international best sellers, debut fiction, and books for kids of all ages to heart-pounding romances, high-velocity thrillers, and stunning science fiction, Amazon Publishing brings outstanding books to a global audience. In 2014, Amazon Publishing was still expanding, but was composed of 14 separate Trade-Mark company trajectories: Logo imprints of all subsidiaries are available at http://www.apub.com/imprints

- **AmazonEncore** — Rediscovered Works

- **AmazonCrossing** — Translated Works

- **Thomas & Mercer** — Mystery, Thrillers, and Suspense

- **Montlake Romance** — Romance

- **47North** — Science Fiction, Fantasy, and Horror

- **Little A** — Literary Fiction

- **Skyscape** — Teen and Young Adult

- **Two Lions** — Children's Picture books, Chapter Books, and Novels

- **Jet City Comics** — Comics and Graphic Novels

- **Lake Union Publishing** — Contemporary and Historical Fiction, Memoir and Popular Nonfiction

- **StoryFront** — Short Fiction

- **Grand Harbor Press** — Personal Growth and Self-Help

- **Waterfall Press** — Christian Nonfiction and Fiction

- **Amazon Publishing** — Nonfiction, Memoirs, and General Fiction

◊Amazon Services LLC

Amazon Services and/or its affiliates ("Amazon") provide website features and other products and services to customers. Authors take advantage of Amazon Web Services, which provides programmatic rights to suppressed features. This convenience began as a communal beta of Amazon Elastic Compute Cloud running Microsoft Windows Server and Microsoft SQL Server. This was later expanded to several operating systems, including various flavors of Linux and OpenSolaris. So when customers visit or shop at Amazon.com, use Amazon products or services, use Amazon applications for mobile, or use software provided by Amazon in connection with any of the foregoing, collectively they all are using Amazon Services LLC. Other services are continuously being added. Presently they include, but not limited to, *Your Profile*, *Gift Cards*, *Service Terms*, *Amazon Instant Video*, Your Media Library, and *mobile applications*.

◊Amazon Student

Amazon Student membership starts once a student fills out a form and their .edu email address is validated. Amazon.com sends an email to the .edu address to verify student eligibility. In 2014 the criteria stated the following..

FREE for 6 months: Get FREE Two-Day Shipping on millions of items, plus exclusive deals, and a credit for each friend you refer. Then for only $49/year after that and...FREE Two-Day Shipping, exclusive deals, & a credit when referring friends. Watch thousands of movies on your laptop, tablet, or phone Become an Amazon Prime member for 50% off (normally $99/yr)

◊Amazon Trademark

Amazon continues buying companies and registering unique names. Their trademarks are a recognizable sign, design and expression which identifies Amazon affiliated products or services of a particular source. Registered trademarks or trade dress of Amazon in the United States and/or other countries may not be used in connection with any product or service that is not

Amazon's, in any manner that is likely to cause confusion among customers, or in any manner that disparages or discredits Amazon.

◊Amazon Vine

Amazon's unique program is called "vine" which is by-invitation only. Members are the most trusted reviewers. Vendors or publishers can submit new or pre-released books for review. A Vine review is unique identified by a green stripe placed adjacent to the Customer review. Book reviewers are also invited to become a Vine-Voice based on the quality and performance of reviews left by that individual.

◊Amazon Webstore

Amazon's services offers website design, shopping-cart functionality, credit card processing, ecommerce hosting, inventory management, and additional features enabling publishers to build online businesses.

○American Bookseller

Description: A monthly journal of the American Booksellers Association (**ABA**) typically promotes independent bookstores in the United States and Canada. In recent years, the journal released the number of new member bookstores to counter other media reports of bookstore closings, with 97 opening in 2006 and over 115 stores opening in 2007.

▪Analytics

Analytics is slang for author's tools that help track various data points in their book. The process provides insight into the success of sales and marketing promotions. Pricing experiments are also part of the analytics game. In self-publishing, these analytics can be provided in near real-time, while traditional publishing delivers semi-annual data or quarterly royalty statements.

○ Anchor Books

Founded in 1953 Anchor Books is the oldest trade paperback publisher in America. The goal was to make inexpensive editions of modern classics widely available to college students and the adult public. Today, Anchor's list boasts award-winning history, science, women's studies, sociology, and quality fiction.

▪Android APK

This industry term refers to a file format. APK is an abbreviation for "application package" and android is an operating system for mobile devices produced by Google. As is the case with many file formats, APK files can have any name needed, provided that the file name ends in ".apk".

▪Anthology

This industry term means a collection of one or more authors published in one single book. More precisely, an anthology is a hand selected compilation or collection of literary works. It could be a collection of poems, short stories, plays, songs, or even excerpts. Genre fiction anthology is a way to categorize collections of small writings such as short stories and short novels, collected into a single volume. A significant compilation or complete collections of works is called *Complete Works*.

○APSS

On January 1, 2013 Brian Jud assumed the position of Executive Director of SPAN, The Small Publishers Association of North America. With the help of previous Executive Director Brad Flora and a new Board of Directors, Jud is making some major changes, not the least of which is changing the name and direction of the association. As if June 1, 2013 SPAN became formally known as The Association of Publishers for Special Sales (**APSS**). The APSS mission is to become known as the premier source of information, education and help for publishers of high-quality content published in printed, electronic or audio form for sale to consumers, non-bookstore retailers and non-retail buyers. APSS intends to become the respected brand-name entity that provides high quality, functional and innovative sales and marketing resources that enhance content producers' efforts to grow their businesses profitably.

▪Artwork

Definition: Drawing or graphics used in various processes to transfer an image onto a substrate. The industry term generally means all illustrative matter not relevant to text.

▪Artisanal

Artisanal publishing is an artistic approach where the book's author takes complete control of writing, crafting, and publishing a high-quality masterpiece.

◊ASIN

ASIN stands for Amazon Standard Identification Number and is the last part of the URL book link (appears after /dp/)

◊Associate

An Amazon Associate is basically a program for referral fee payments. Payment amounts and more information on payments is available in Associates Central under Account Settings. View payment history at the following website link.............................

https://associates.amazon.com/gp/associates/network/your-account/payment-history.html.

▪As Told To

The slang expression explains a book produced by a writer in collaboration with a non-writer. Most certainly, the non-writer is noteworthy like a celebrity.

○Audiobooks

An audiobook is a recording of a text being read. It wasn't until the 1980s that this medium began to attract book retailers. Bookstores began displaying audiobooks on bookshelves rather than in separate displays.The industry makes and identifies two categories. A reading of the complete text is noted as "unabridged", while readings of a reduced version of the text are labeled as "abridged". Audiobook production is encouraged for independent authors. The cost saving DIY (doing it yourself) route is not the best way but tools are available.

◊Audible Author Services

Amazon.com's online portal is used by authors to connect with Audible (an Amazon company that markets audio book versions). The program can only be used by authors listed on a book. A publishing company cannot sign up for services on an author's behalf. Audible also provides a service that enables authors to post their books where producers and narrators can bid for the audio rights to the works.

▪Author

Definition: The industry term is most always refers to a person who originated or gave existence to anything written. Essentially, an identity is assigned when determining responsibility for what was created. Narrowly defined, an author is the originator of any written work and can also be described as a writer.

◊Author Central

Amazon.com created a portal allowing authors to control their personal information appearing on a bio-page. Information can be entered such as related works, photos, blogs, videos, tours, and biographical information. Analytics were added and made available as well. Through *BookScan*, sales tracking and rankings are possible.

▪Author-Services

Businesses that advertise consultation for authors are companies that help in the self-publishing efforts and provide editing services, cover design, and management of resellers.

○Author Solutions

The publishing mega-giant, Penguin, recently acquired Author Solutions. This parent company of multiple self-publishing imprints, includes: iUniverse, Wordclay, AuthorHouse, Xlibris, AuthorHive, Trafford, Palibrio, and Hollywood Pitch.

○Authors Guild

Description: The membership organization is a not-for-profit American society of and for authors. It has around eight thousand members, among them published authors, literary agents and attorneys who mainly deal in book publishing. It provides members with free legal and business advice on book contracts, periodical and literary agency contracts, subsidiary licensing, royalty and copyright issues and other matters relevant to publishing. It has been involved in conflicts with Google and Amazon. The guild is responsible for The Western States Book Awards (annually) for fiction, creative nonfiction, and poetry designed to increase sales and critical attention nationally for fine literary works.

◊Author Rank

Amazon Author Rank is the definitive list of best-selling authors on Amazon.com. This list makes it easy for readers to discover the best-selling authors on Amazon.com overall and within a selection of major genres. Amazon Author Rank is your rank based on the sales of all of your books on Amazon.com. Just like Amazon Best Sellers, it is updated hourly. The top 100 authors overall and the top 100 in selected genres will be displayed on Amazon.com. You can see your Amazon Author Rank trended over time in Author Central. You can find your Amazon Author Rank in Author Central under the Rank tab.

▪Autograph Party

The expression is commonly used by bookstores when there's an anticipated gathering where the author personally signs customers' purchased books. Author's signatures are a form of product promotion and the bookstore party is a staged event to attract potential customers. The facility supplies the venue and the author attracts the audience.

▪AutoResponder

An **autoresponder** is a computer program that automatically answers an e-mail sent to it. They are often used as e-mail marketing tools, which immediately provides information to prospective customers and then follows-up at preset time intervals. An autoresponder sequence can do amazing things for a book business, but there's a risk every time a product is pitched to subscribers. Done incorrectly, the marketing campaign could hurt the overall relationship.

◊AWS

AWS stands for Amazon Web Services. AWS hosts many internet companies and government agencies like Netflix, reddit, Spotify, and Central Intelligence Agency. Amazon Web Services (AWS) provides Amazon's developer customers with access to in-the-cloud infrastructure services based on Amazon's own back-end technology platform, which developers can use to enable virtually any type of business. Some examples of the services offered by Amazon Web Services: Amazon Elastic Compute Cloud (Amazon EC2) • Amazon Simple Storage Service (Amazon S3) • Amazon SimpleDB • Amazon Simple Queue Service (Amazon SQS) • Amazon Flexible Payments Service (Amazon FPS) • Amazon Mechanical Turk • Amazon CloudFront.

2 B-B

B

▪Backend

The industry term refers to promoting a book publication to blogs, newsletters, and other books. Generally, the more appropriate media would be e-books where active Internet links can take the reader directly to the targeted product. The campaign is done at the back-end, more or less encouraging further reading, word of mouth publicity, or buying related products. Affiliate programs earn money too, like Amazon Associates where they can get commissions if someone buys something from Amazon through their created unique link in a book or website.

▪Back flap

The back flap refers to the inside panel of a dust jacket covering a hardcover book. Often the back flaps are printed with biographical information about the author, a summary of the book from the publisher (known as a blurb), and/or critical praise from celebrities or authorities.

▪Backlight

Backlighting is the light assembly in an ebook that is behind the text enabling people to read in poor light or in the dark. The major reason why many manufactures don't incorporate a backlit screen is because of how much the luxury device decreases battery life.

▪Backlist

Previously published books that are still in print and available from a publisher are called backlists. This term means the opposite to front-list (newly published) books.

▪Back Matter

All books have back pages which are called back matter, similar to a sandwich that has a piece of bread on the top and bottom to hold the ingredients inside. Traditionally, the back matter consists of four distinct areas. Page A is the appendix (or appendices). Page B can be the bibliography or recommended reading. Page C becomes the glossary, if included. Page D is the index. Page E could be the colophon which details the production facts about the book, such as the computer and word processing system. A final page may be an order form for obtaining additional books etc.

▪Bad Break

Bad break is an illogical or unpleasant-looking beginning or end of a page already printed on one side. It also refers to a hyphen in the wrong place in a word.

▪Banner Ad

Banner ad is a form of advertising that embeds an advertisement onto a Web page. When visitors click on the ad they go to the sponsor's Web site, called click-through. Typically, banners are delivered by a central ad server. The system works automatically, but a simple explanation is when the advertiser's log-files are scanned, web user visitors are detected on the advertiser's site. A further detection occurs when the visitor clicks on the banner ad. If a purchase is completed, the advertiser sends the content provider some small amount of money (usually around five to ten US cents). This payback system is often how the content provider is able to pay for the Internet access to supply the content in the first place. Usually though, advertisers use ad networks to serve their advertisements, resulting in a revenue share system and higher quality ad placement.

○Bantam Books

Random House, the German media corporation subsidiary of Bertelsmann, owns Bantam Books (an imprint of the Random House Publishing Group). The American publishing house was founded in 1945 by Walter B. Pitkin, Jr., Sidney B. Kramer, and Ian and Betty Ballantine. It started as a mass market publisher, mostly of reprints of hardcover books, with some original paperbacks. It expanded into trade paperback and hardcover original works, often reprinted in house as mass market editions.

Bantam has published the original editions of the "Choose Your Own Adventure" series of children's books, as well as the first original novels based on the dozen Star Trek stories between 1970 and 1982 when the license was sold to Pocket Books. Bantam also published a dozen volumes of short story scripts from Star Trek: The Original Series. Bantam is also the American paperback publisher of The Guinness Book of Records.

■Bar Code

A Bar Code is the *Bookland* **EAN** scanning symbol (code) that goes on the back book cover. The symbol allows an optical scanning tool to identify the title, International Standard Book Number (ISBN), and price for an individual product. In the case of music or film products, the bar code will also identify the Universal Product Code (UPC). Ideally, bar codes should be integrated into the design. If a book cover is not customized, the designer can obtain a film master or EPS file from the bar code production company. In most cases this film master or EPS file can then be integrated into the product's back cover. Another option, if a book has already been printed, bar code labels can be applied to the back cover of each book. That way, labels can be removed by the customer. The presence of bar codes on books and products are a significant factor in determining how quickly shipments are received, and therefore how consistently a title is in inventory and available to Amazon's customers. For this reason, Amazon.com requires that products shipped to fulfillment centers include a bar code image.

○Barns & Noble

After a series of mergers and bankruptcies in the American bookstore industry starting in the 1990s, Barnes & Noble, a Fortune 500 company, stands as America's only national bookstore chain and the largest retail bookseller in the United States. The enterprise is also the leading retailer of content, digital media and educational products in the country. The company operates 663 retail stores in all 50 U.S. states in addition to 696 college bookstores that serve more than 4.6 million students and faculty members across the country. Barnes & Noble also operates one of the Web's largest e-commerce sites, BN.com. The worldwide bookseller/store created the Nook ebook device.

○ **BEA**

The BEA (BookExpo America) is the number one book and author event in the United States. In 2014, BEA returned to three full days of Exhibits and four full days of Conferences with Special Events at the Javits Center in New York City.

○ **Beacon Press**

Not to be confused with Beacon Hill Press of Kansas City (a NPH imprint), Beacon Press is an American non-profit book publisher. Founded in 1854 by the American Unitarian Association, it is currently a department of the Unitarian Universalist Association.

▪ **Beat**

A beat is a general term in writing that identifies a piece of action. Many times, creative writing employs this in place of a *tag*. Professional writers claim it awkward and wordy to use both a beat and a tag. Occasionally this basic rule can be broken for effect, but generally, the rule is that it should be done purposefully, in terms of rhythm or pacing. Example: *"Your cat is ugly," aunt Lela claimed, patting poor Sara on the back.* There's no benefit in writing this way. Tighter writing is better. *Lela patted poor Sara on the back. "Your cat is ugly."*

○Belknap Press

HUP (Harvard University Press) owns the Belknap Press imprint, which it inaugurated in May 1954 with the publication of the Harvard Guide to American History. The John Harvard Library book series is published under the Belknap imprint.

■Benday

This industry term describes various density screens printed on an adhesive-backed plastic sheet that may be pasted to artwork. Though current technology replaces this method, the screening provides tonal qualities. Named after illustrator and printer Benjamin Henry Day, Jr., the technique dates back to 1879. The printing process is called Ben-Day dots which differ from halftone dots in that they are always of equal size and distribution in a specific area. To apply the dots to a drawing the artist would purchase transparent overlay sheets from a stationery supplier, available in a wide variety of dot size and distribution, which gave the artist a range of tones to use in the work. The overlay material was cut in the shapes of the tonal areas desired—i.e. shadow or background or surface treatment and rubbed onto the specific areas of the drawing with a burnishing tool. When photographically reproduced as a line cut for letterpress printing, the areas of Ben-Day overlay provided tonal shading to the printing plate.

■Best Seller

The phrase means top-selling book. There are several best seller lists that draw sales figures from various markets. The popular lists compiled weekly are by *The New York Times*, *Publishers Weekly*, and *Time*.

▪Best Selling Authors

Generally speaking, the number one reason to buy a book is because of the author. Becoming a favorite is based on certain factors, like popularity, recognizable name, world status, talents, etc. In 2014, the popular rankings in order were… James Patterson, Stephen King, Janent Evanovich, John Grishham, Jeff Kinney, Bill O'Reilly, Nora Roberts, Daniel Steel, Suzanne Collins, Dean Koontz, J.K. Rowling, George Martin, Stephanie Meyer, Ken Follet, and Rick Riordan.

▪Beta Tester

A beta tester is a person who reads a particular book before the commercial release and offers constructive feedback to the author. The industry coined term evolved from the Beta phase following the Alpha phase of software testing. Testers were usually customers or prospective customers willing to test the software without charge, often receiving the final software free or for a reduced price.

◊Betterizer

The **Betterizer** replaced the "improve your recommendations" link. But replacing the actual "Amazon" recommendations seems to be a major complaint. When someone sees an item of interest, they simply click the "Like" button below the item. Amazon will then note it, and show another item that they hope the consumer may also like.

If someone is not sure, for example, about an item and wants to learn more before selecting "Like", they hover over the image to see more details. If they don't see anything of interest, the "Refresh and show different items" link is clicked to see a whole new set of items.

▪Bibliography

A back matter listing includes books and materials consulted by the author in the book preparation. The references are included for additional subject material to bring to the reader's attention.

○ Big Six

Big Six is a slang expression commonly used in the book world. Random House is considered one of the "Big Six" publishing companies, along with Hachette, Macmillan, Penguin, HarperCollins, and Simon & Schuster.

▪Binding Options

A major decision in production is the book binding. There are many factors that can help in making a decision. A sourcebook that readers will be in and out of many times usually requires a hard cover (frequently referred to as cloth or casebound) which is durable. The Cadillac hardcover bindings are Smythe sewn. In this technique, thread is used to stitch the signatures before glued into the cover. For a top quality production book, headbands and foot-bands are utilized. They are small reinforcing strips of cloth added to the top and bottom. Perfect, or adhesive, binding is another method – and currently the most popular. In this process, the signatures are collated, run through hot adhesive, and then affixed to the cover. It is frequently used because it gives a spine surface area and is the least expensive of quality bindings.

○BISAC

BISAC stands for Book Industry Systems Advisory Committee; a committee of the Book Industry Study Group (BISG), a U.S. trade association for policy, technical standards and research related to books and similar products. The objective is to simplify logistics for publishers, manufacturers, suppliers, wholesalers, retailers, librarians and others involved in the business of print and electronic media.

○**Bitly Brand Tools**

This convenience is a must-have for marketers to fuel branding, engagement, and understanding in the connected world. (http://www.bitly.com): Bitly helps save & share interesting things discovered on the web. Consumers are encouraged to check out their knowledge base for details and to provide feedback.

A free account is possible. The idea is to copy and paste a book's link into where it says "Paste link here". When done, BITLY will give a shortened link that can be used to link the book. Publisher's will want to place this shortened link inside books when cross-promoting them. When they again login to BITLY, they will also be able to see the stats for the posted links, such as how many "clicks" they have (the number of people that have been clicking on the links for a book).

With link, people can copy or write it down and type it into their browser. When viewed on a Kindle device, they don't have a web browser to view the recommended website. That's why some may write it down.

•Save a link to any page, image, song or video. Just paste the URL into the box at the top right of the page.

•Easily share your bitmarks on Facebook, Twitter, or via email.

•Check on your stats to see how your bitmarks fared on the interwebs.

▪Bitmarks

Description: A **Bitly** term describing a search feature with enhancement. The better bookmarks save, search, and organize all links from around the web. Publishers can also group them into bundles. Authors can share them with friends. If not wanted on a particular public profile, the user marks them as private.

○Black Lizard

Vintage Crime/Black Lizard was founded in June 1990 after Random House's acquisition of the publishing company created by Donald S. Ellis and Barry Gifford. Before the purchase, Vintage Books was publishing the work of American mystery-authors such as Dashiell Hammett, James M. Cain and Raymond Chandler under the Vintage Crime label. As a result of the alliance, Random House came into the possession of the literature of Jim Thompson and David Goodis, along with that of many other noir writers. Vintage Crime/Black Lizard is one of the preeminent publishers of crime fiction in the United States and asserts that it remains devoted to the best of "classic crime", having added Eric Ambler, Chester Himes and Ross Macdonald to their list of authors.

▪Bleed

A bleed is ink printed over the edge of the paper. The edge is trimmed off. Magazines usually have covers with bleed. It is very difficult to print exactly to the edge of a sheet of paper/card so, to accommodate this, it becomes necessary to print a larger area than needed and trim the medium used down to the required final size. Images, backgrounds and fills which are intended to go to the edge must be extended beyond the trim line to give a bleed.

Bleeds in the USA generally are 1/8 of an inch from where the cut is made. In the UK and Europe, they generally are 2 to 5mm from where the cut occurs. This varies from one print company to another. Some ask for specific sizes and place the specified demands on their website or offer templates that are already set to their required bleed settings.

▪Blog

A blog is a website (web-log truncation) or basically a discussion or informational site published on the World Wide Web. Individuals or groups record information and opinions on subject matter. Most are considered discrete entries or posts. Typically they are displayed in reverse chronological order (the most recent post appears first). Blogs were initially intended to be the work of a single individual. Then, occasionally a small group covered a single subject. Recently "multi-author blogs" (MABs) have developed. Posts are getting more sophisticated and written by large numbers of authors and professionally edited. Blog can also be used as a verb, meaning to maintain or add content to a blog. A blog can be a fantastic platform to build a business around, the kind of flexible business you can run on your terms from anywhere in the world. Your blog can bring a perfect place to explore your creative side. Writing, video, podcasting, graphics... a blog can be the central hub of your creations. Don't go searching for that dream job, though. Start a blog, become a blogger, and demonstrate expertise and passion for the job desired. Authors don't need a publisher these days to build a successful writing career. Writers are using blogs to launch careers, build followings and earn a living.

▪Blueline

Description: The printing process for copying using the diazo chemical process (blue lines on a white background), also known as whiteprint A blueline is a proof sheet made by exposing a negative to a photosensitive paper (opposite of blueprint). The printing industry seldom uses this process anymore.

▪Blurb

A blurb is a short promotion; a description praising a book, for example, so people will want to buy it. Usually, the blurb is like an advertisement that appears on the back cover of a book. Some people independently provide blurbs and are known as blurbers.

▪Boards

A slang expression meaning a pasted up copy is camera-ready for the printer. Boards are the backing for the camera-ready materials like photostats and line art that is attached with adhesive. Once a page was complete, the board would be attached to an easel and photographed in order to create a negative, which was then used to make a printing plate.

▪Body Type

The majority of the typeface used in a book that is not a headline. Fontfeed.com is an excellent source for recommended fonts, typography techniques, and inspirational examples of digital type.

▪Boldface

Definition: Type that is heavier than the text type with which it is used.

▪Bond

Description: A hard finish rag or sulphite paper generally used for stationary and forms. Bond paper is durable and similar to bank paper but having a weight greater than 50 g/m2. The name comes from documents like government **bonds**. It is generally used as paper for electronic printers. Widely employed for graphic work involving pencil, pen and felt-tip marker, bond paper can sometimes contain rag fibre pulp, which produces a stronger, though rougher, sheet of paper.

▪Book

By definition, a book is a publication consisting of 49 or more pages that is not a serial or periodical. When less than 49 pages, the smaller book is called a booklet.

▪Book Clubs

Description: BOMC or Book of the Month Club is probably the largest and most popular but there are many niche clubs that serve specific audiences. For example, Book discussion clubs are basically a group of people who meet to discuss books they have read. Interestingly, there's also specific club subjects like the Movie and Entertainment Book Club, Conservative Book Club, Teen Age Book Club, Writer's Digest Book Club, Spiritual Book Associates, Rodale's Organic Gardening Book Club, Metaphysical Book Club, The Military Book Club, and many more.

■Book Half Title

Description: A page inside of a book that only has the book's title is called a book half title; sometimes called a bastard title.

■Book Handle

Description: Unlike a blurb, a book handle is a succinct response that elicits intrigue and appeal. It is composed of 20 to 30 words that captures the essence of a book and make people think, "I want that."

■Book Packager

Description: A person or company who contracts with publishers to deliver contracted books. A book-packaging company acts as a link between a publisher and the writers, researchers, editors, and designers that produce the book. Thus, they tend to amalgamate the roles of agent, editor, and publisher. A book-packager is more common in the fiction market, particularly for books aimed at pre-teens and teenagers, and in the illustrated non-fiction co-edition market.

■Book Post

Description: The Postal Service's book rate (media mail and special rate). Generally used for books (at least eight pages), film

(16 mm or narrower), printed music, printed test materials, sound recordings, play scripts, printed educational charts, loose-leaf pages and binders consisting of medical information, and computer-readable media. Advertising restrictions apply. Packages must measure 108 in. or less in combined length and girth.

○ Book Sense

The **ABA** sponsors this marketing program (BookSence.com). It is intended to preserve a connection between consumers and local independent bookstores. In June 2008, the company was bought by *IndieBound*. It is now a different and new program based website.

■ Book Series

The expression refers to a series of books created by publishing another book that is relevant to a particular current book. This way, when someone reads the book, the publisher will be able to direct them to buy and download the next book also. This gives the publisher an opportunity to make more money from their books on the back-end.

○ BookBaby

Description: This industry coined word describes a person or business that manages an author's Barnes & Nobel, Apple, or Amazon accounts. A BookBaby charges an up-front fee based on the level of service, but pays the 100 percent collected royalties to the author.

▪Bookmark

Description: Often used as an inexpensive promotional piece, a bookmark is simply a rectangular slip for keeping a place in a book. Bookmarks are also links to websites that make it easy to get back to a favorite place. It technically is a Uniform Resource Identifier (**URI**) stored for later retrieval in various storage formats. Web browsers include bookmark features called *favorites* or Internet shortcuts, and by virtue of that browser's large market share, these terms have been synonymous with bookmark since the first browser war. Bookmarks are normally accessed through a menu in the user's web browser, and folders are commonly used for organization.

▪BookMarking

Description: The expression refers to a feature that enables readers to tag important pages inside an ebook.

◊Book-Ology

Amazon Trademark; Amazon.com developed Bookology in partnership with University Games. It's a game for anyone who loves books. So, for a well-read board game player or a bookworm who loves to play games, Bookology is sure to offer both challenges and entertainment. (For two or more players; ages 12 and older)

◊Bookranking

Amazon and other sellers use benchmarks to keep track of a book's popularity progress. There are tracking tools authors use. An example is http//www.sellbox.com/book-sales where progress is monitored along with a sales analysis. Good marketers become better when they can determine what happens to sales when the price changes, what advertising works, changing the cover design, promotions, publicity campaign, and book tours. Valuable historical information doesn't begin to accumulate until publishers register the books to track (including competitive books). Amazon's warning is, "Don't wait because you can always abandon your use of a tool. Most are free or free for a limited period of time so register and see which works best for your situation."

There are free and valuable book registrars to use as an effective tool. Listed in alphabetical order, they are Amazon Author Rank/AuthorCentral, Books & Writers, eBook Tracker, Metric Junkie, NovelRank, rankforest, RankTracer, Sales Rank Express, and TrackerBox.

○ Books on Tape

Description: The slang expression is actually a business, a division of Random House that sells unabridged audiobooks.

○ BookScan

BookScan is a division of the Nielsen ratings company. They provide data analytics for the book-publishing industry and report sales results of book retailers across the United States.

◊ Bookshelf

Description: The Bookshelf is where an author can view all of his or hers published books and make new ones.

◊Booksleuth

Amazon Trademark (biblio.com) specializes in Reference, Religion, and Textbooks. It is the largest independent marketplace for sellers today who work with thousands of independent bookstores and booksellers around the world. Together they offer nearly 100 million used and rare books for sale.

◊BookSurge

The Amazon company was an early author-services business that has now become part of CreateSpace.

▪BookTalk

Booktalk.org is an online community where users discuss books and take part in live chats and interviews with authors.

▪Book Trailer

Description: Trailer refers to a video ad and can be used to publicize a book. The technique is similar to movie trailers and circulated online.

○BookWire

Bookwire (by Bowker) is a mobile app for your iPhone that gives you the ability to scan a barcode or enter the ISBN, access book records, and add titles to wish lists.

○Borders

Borders Group, Inc. (former NYSE ticker symbol BGP) once was an international book and music retailer based in Ann Arbor,

Michigan employing 19,500 throughout the U.S., primarily in its Borders and Waldenbooks stores. The company filed for bankruptcy in early 2011. Borders was not able to find a buyer with the last remaining stores closing their doors on Sunday, September 18, 2011. Rival Barnes & Noble acquired Borders' trademarks and customer list and their former website was replaced by a redirect to Barnes & Noble's.

○**Bowker**

Description: R.R. **Bowker**, the United States publishing industry support company, is the official US ISBN agency and has contracts with agents, such as Publisher Services, to assist self-publishers obtain official identification links and bar codes.

▪**Boxed**

Description: A special technique used for drawing attention to a certain paragraph or feature by enclosing it inside a precise rectangular graphic.

▪**Brick and Mortar**

Brick and Mortar (also bricks and mortar or B&M) in its simplest usage describes the physical presence of a building(s) or other structure. The slang term is often used to refer to a company that possesses buildings or store for operations. The name is a suitable substitution resulting from traditional building materials like bricks and mortar. The reference was originally coined by Charles Dickens in the book *Little Dorrit*.

More precisely, in the verbiage of e-commerce, brick-and-mortar businesses have a physical presence offering face-to-face customer experiences. This term is more than likely used to contrast a transitory business or an internet-only presence, such as an online shop, which may have no physical presence for shoppers to visit and buy from directly. Online businesses normally have non-public physical facilities from which they either run business operations, and/or warehousing for mass physical product storage and distribution. Concerns for foot traffic, storefront visibility, and appealing design apply only to brick-and-mortar outlets rather than online businesses.

▪Bulk

Bulk means the thickness of paper in number of pages per inch (PPI). The term also refers to the thickness of a book, not counting the cover. Used as a verb, bulk means to make a book appear thicker than what the amount of text would otherwise require by using thicker paper.

▪Bulleted List

The term refers to an important writing aspect; a way of organizing long sections of text by pointing out specific topics.

▪Buffer

Description: A website to schedule Twitter, Facebook, and LinkedIn posts.

▪Buzz

Buzz is a slang industry term which means speculative or excited talk and discussions that centers on generating word-of-mouth publicity (good or bad) for a book.

■Buzzstorming

Buzzstorming is an industry slang word which simply means brainstorming to promote a book title. Internet forums are many, where publishers can join to read ideas about how others promote books. The premise is that the more help from others, the more success. The online community strikes a friendly tone and offers good advice for writers looking for unconventional or interesting ways to market work.

3 C-C

C

C1S

Description: Industry term which means Coated One Side referring to a book cover stock that is smooth on one side.

Calibre

Calibre is a free, open-source ebook-management tool available for Macintosh, Windows, and Linux that can import and export many formats.

Calligraphy

The hand lettering technique is often ornate and occasionally used for poetry and cookbooks in particular.

Camera Ready Copy

A completely prepared paste-up that is ready for the camera or reproduction. No further graphic arts work is required at this stage.

○Cameron Belt Press

The state-of-the-art printer is used by a few book manufacturers. The press can slice a big chunk off large quantity book runs (especially on orders of more than 10,000). Huge quantities isn't always good and not recommended for self-publishers. Also, the belt press does not comply with the standard 16-32 page signature rules. Each trim size has a unique signature.

◊Camp NaNoWriMo

Inspired by the NaNoWriMo 50,000-word novel in 30 days challenge, Camp NaNoWriMo occurs annually for a writer's retreat. https://campnanowrimo.org/sign_in.

▪Caption

Caption is the line of text that accompanies an illustration.

▪Captured Keystroke

Description: A slang computer user term meaning the information, once entered, is retained by the computer and therefore does not need retyping.

▪Case Binding

Description: The technical term simply refers to a hardcover book. Case-bound means the hardcover or edition binding.

▪Castoff

Definition: An estimate of the manuscript length when typeset.

▪Catalog Sheet

Description: A promotional page including contents, author, discounts, and a book's vital statistics.

▪Cataloging-in-Publication Data

Description: An industry phrase explaining the bibliographic information supplied by the Library of Congress that is printed on the copyright page. The **CIP** data helps libraries shelve the book properly.

○**CBA**

CBA stands for Christian Bookseller Association, a trade association of religious bookstores and suppliers. The CBA Best-Seller and category top-seller lists are compiled from actual sales in Christian stores as reported through CROSS:SCAN.

▪Center Spread

Definition: The pair of facing pages in the center of a book or magazine. The term also means a feature that occupies the center pages of a magazine or newspaper.

▪Chain

The publishing chain is both supply and value. As a supply chain it provides a series of organizational links by means of which a specific book is gradually produced and transmitted via distributors and retailers to an end user. There's also a value chain in the sense that each of the links purportedly adds some value in the process.

▪ChapBook

The publication is a small pamphlet of popular tales, ballads or poems. The term also refers to present-day publications, usually poetry, of up to about 40 pages, ranging from low-cost productions to expensive, finely produced editions.

▪Character

Definition: The letters, numbers, and punctuation marks or space in printed materials.

▪Chat

Description: An online discussion group or forum.

▪Check Digit

Description: The number used to validate other numerals in the ISBN. The last number is the check digit, in this case.

▪Checking Copy

Description: The first published books are the finished books sent to a prepublication (galley) reviewer.

▪Chicago Manual of Style

The expression describes a comprehensive, authoritative source on writing style and a unique process for writers, editors, and publishers.

▪Circles

Basically, the slang term refers to groups who might check out what books are hot, usually at institutions of higher learning. Circles provide insider information and what book leads the pack at one of the circles which can then be classified as a best-seller.

▪Circling

Circling is the act of establishing a connection between two people on Google+. The term is closely synonymous with "following," and "friending" on Twitter and Facebook.

○CJ (formaly Commision Junction)

Affiliate by Conversant (by CONVERSANT) is now **CJ**, the former Commission Junction. This leading global affiliate marketing network, specializes in pay-for-performance programs that drive results for businesses around the world. The **CJ** Network helps to reach and connect with millions of online consumers every day by facilitating productive partnerships between advertisers and publishers, drive more sales and expand reach. Five students from the University of California Santa Barbara establish Commission Junction®, in 1998. **CJ** is now the number one affiliate marketing provider in the world. http://www.cj.com

▪Clean Copy

Description: The galley or manuscript that is free from correction marks, deletions, and other unnecessary notations.

○ ClickBank

The business is an online retailer that enables authors to sell ebooks directly by creating an account, uploading the files, pricing them, and selling.

Click-Through Rate

A measurement based on a percentage of Web users who click on a targeted advertisement. This technique provides information about the ad's effectiveness.

Clip Art

Description: The line drawings, screened pictures and illustrations designed to be cut out and pasted up.

Clipping Service

Description: The person or firm that collects articles of particular interest for a client from periodicals.

Cloth

Definition: The material used for binding or casing of books.

Coated Stock

Description: Paper that is manufactured with a variety of surfaces, that may be smooth, glossy or matte. Coated paper has a thin layer of material such as calcium carbonate or china clay applied to one or both sides in order to create a surface more suitable for high-resolution halftone screens. (Uncoated papers are rarely suitable for screens above 150 lpi.) Coated or uncoated papers may have their surfaces polished by calendering. Coated papers are divided into matte, semi-matte or silk, and gloss.

▪Collating

Definition: The gathering of printed sheets into proper order for binding. The advantage is that it makes assembly fast and easy for a user to find an element confirm it is absent from the list. In automatic systems this is done using a computerized interpolation search.

▪Colophon

Definition: The listing of production details in the back matter. Colophon is a Greek word that means "finishing touches."

▪Color Correction

The method uses masking, dot etching, re-etching, and scanning to improve color rendition.

▪Color Printing

Definition: Any printing of color, other than black on white paper. One example is three-color printing using three different ink colors.

▪Color Separation

Description: The camera technique that uses various color lenses to bring out three primary colors along with black from an illustration or photo. The negative that results is called a film separation or sep negs and are used in making printing plates.

▪Comb Binding

Description: The book binding technique that uses a plastic multipronged device allowing a book to lie flat when opened. The assembly is sometimes referred to as cerlox or surelox and is one of many ways to bind pages together into a book. The comb method uses round plastic spines with 19 rings (for US Letter size) or 21 rings (for A4 size) and a hole puncher that makes rectangular holes. Comb binding is sometimes referred to as plastic comb binding or spiral comb binding.

▪Composition

Description: The typeset material and text ready to be pasted up.

▪Compositor

Description: A person who sets type is a typesetter or compositor.

◊Content Creators

Content creation is the formation of information, especially digital content, for self-expression, distribution, marketing and/or publication. Typical forms of content creation include maintaining and updating web sites, blogging, photography, videography, online commentary, the maintenance of social media accounts, and editing and distribution of digital media. Amazon drives innovation by sanctioning content creators as well as consumers and sellers. Kindle Direct Publishing and Amazon Publishing give authors innovative means to bring books to readers. Amazon Studios is developing feature films and episodic series in a new way, one that's open to great ideas from creators and audiences around the world. CreateSpace makes it simple to print and distribute books, music, and video through Internet retail outlets, personal websites, bookstores, retailers, libraries, and academic institutions--on-demand.

▪Content Editing

Content editing means reviewing a manuscript and making it more appealing by suggesting revisions to content, organization, structure, and style.

▪Continuity Program

Description: The standing order for succeeding volumes in a related program.

▪Conversion

Conversion is a process that transforms a book from one format to another.

▪Cookie

A cookie is sometimes referred to as an HTTP cookie, web cookie, or browser cookie. It is a small piece of data that's sent from a website and stored in a user's web browser. This all takes place when the user is browsing that website. When on the Internet, every time a particular website is loaded, the browser sends the cookie back to the server to record and notify the website of the user's previous activity. Cookies were designed to be a reliable mechanism for websites to remember marketable information or to record the user's browsing activity. The technology basically works with web browsers to store information like user preferences, login information, and shopping cart contents.

▪Co-op Advertising

Description: The publisher and bookstore shares in this publicity method.

▪Co-op Money

Description: A bookstore publicity event may have an events coordinator who will normally ask for a portion of the funds necessary to promote the celebration. This is referred to in the industry as co-op money which is essentially matching promotional funds paid by the publisher to booksellers.

▪Co-op Publishing

The industry term refers to one person or company joining with another to produce a book and sometimes called co-publishing.

▪Copyediting

Copyediting is simply the process of correcting spelling errors, and improving grammar, style, and factual accuracy in a manuscript.

◊Copyright

COPYRIGHT is where all content included in or made available through any Amazon Service, such as text, graphics, logos, button icons, images, audio clips, digital downloads, and data compilations is the property of Amazon or its content suppliers and protected by United States and international copyright laws. The compilation of all content included in or made available through any Amazon Service is the exclusive property of Amazon and protected by U.S. and international copyright laws.

▪Copyright

Copyright means the exclusive legal right to reproduce, publish, sell, or distribute material as in a literary or artistic work. Copyrights protect original creative works such as paintings, songs, books, photographs and other original works of authorship. With a federal copyright registration the originator can control who may copy, use and distribute the work and enforce the copyright in federal court.

▪Copyright Notice

The words are placed on the copyright page, such as "Copyright © 2015, CadArm Publications."

▪Copywriting

Copywriting is an essential element of effective online marketing. The art and science of direct-response copywriting involves strategically delivering words (whether written or spoken) that gets people to take action. It's an art because it requires creativity, a sense of style, a certain aptitude, mastery, and special knowledge. The process is oriented so the creative content is marketing that's not just practical and persuasive, but awe-inspiring and breathtaking. Writing effective copy is also a science, because it exists in the world of tests, trials and failures, improvements, breakthroughs, education and predictability. It may even be considered scientific advertising because it develops ideas and then tests that idea. It's how to know if content marketing is working. In bad copy, one (or both) of these elements are missing. In good copy, these important ingredients are both abundant.

◊Community

A community is a section consisting of an online forum where one can interact with other publishers. This is useful for asking questions and how things work.

◊Consumers

Technological innovation drives the growth of Amazon.com to offer customers more types of products, more conveniently and at lower prices. Since 1995, Amazon has significantly expanded its product selection, international retail websites, and worldwide network of fulfillment and customer service centers, offering everything from toys and video games to MP3 downloads and collectible items. The company entered the e-book hardware industry in 2007 with the release of the original Kindle reader. The Kindle family has now grown to include Kindle Fire HD 4G LTE Wireless, with HD display, Dolby Digital Plus, and 4G connectivity; and Kindle Paperwhite, the world's most advanced e-reader.

▪Costs to Publish

Description: One huge question that currently haunts self-publishers is in comparing prices for traditional ink-press printing, PQN (Print Quantity Needed) and POD (Print-On-Demand, one book at a time such as DocuTech). For comparison, the comparative example used is a softcover (perfect bound) 144 page 5.5 x 8.5 book with black text and a four-color cover.

1. Press (ink on paper): **$1.55** each but must print at least 3,000 to get a price this low. So, the print bill will be $4,650. (2014)

2. Digital printer (short run): 500 copies for $2.80 each for a print bill of $1,400, or 100 copies for **$5.17** each and a print bill of $517.

3. POD (single copies): May run **$6 to $10** and are often bundled with other services. Print-On-Demand is a good option when a book has run its course, inventory is exhausted, but still receive orders for a couple of copies a month. Rather than invest in inventory, supplier can have books made one-at-a-time as needed.

◊Cover Image

Description: A book is judged by its cover! A cover image can have a direct impact on a readers' purchasing decisions and adding a high quality cover image is an effective way to inspire customer confidence and boost sales. Go to…

(https://kdp.amazon.com/help?topicId=A2J0TRG6OPX0VM)

for help in formatting and uploading a cover image. There are a number of obstacles to overcome and it certainly is beneficial to not add to the problem with amateur looking book covers. Good advice is to go to a freelancing site like Elance.com or Odesk.com and hire a professional designer. Industry practice employs five general rules concerning a cover image. The first task is to find multiple examples of great cover designs as examples. Next, instruct the designer to make sure the title stands out. Photographs must also be extremely eye-catching that evokes a powerful emotion. Usually, the crop size is 1880 x 2500 width-to-length (best size for Amazon). The final proof is shrunk down to 90 pixels wide (the thumbnail size that's on many of Amazon's promotions). It's getting harder every day to get noticed in the Amazon crowded marketplace. The cover is the only way to catch someone's attention.

▪CPM

CPM means Cost Per Mille which is basically the marketing cost per thousand views; a means of measuring certain print advertising.

▪CPU

CPU stands for Central Processing Unit and generally refers to the microprocessor and computer memory. The term is carried over from the mini computer world industry.

◊CreateSpace

Amazon Trademark website that utilizes innovative free tools and top-notch professional services making publishing and distribution easier than ever. Plus it pays to self-publish with CreateSpace. Their royalty structure provides industry-leading economics, putting more in an author's pocket. Manufacturing and shipping is all taken care of and the book remains in-stock, without inventory, because it is made on-demand when customers order. And with an array of options, including a free Interior Reviewer and Cover Creator, together the author and publisher can create the book professionally for free. Plus, the book is made available through Amazon.com and many other distribution options.

▪Crane

Description: An industry slang word meaning a prepublication galley.

▪Critique Circle

Description: A free online collaborative-writing workshop for all genres with an extensive array of features.

▪Critters Workshop

Description: A member of the Critique.org family of online workshops/critique groups for writers of science fiction, fantasy, and horror.

▪Crop Marks

Sometimes called trim marks, crop marks are lines used to define the desired limits of the area of a photograph or illustration to be reproduced.

▪Cropping

A photo or illustration generally needs proportion adjustments prior to insertion. Placing pencil marks at the margins and corners indicates what the proportion needs to be so the object can be reproduced accordingly.

▪Cross-Promotion

Future books can be cross-promoted and done within the current book that's published. One way is to add a chapter "Preview of next book". Or a section in the book might be called "Check Out My Other Books."

▪CrowdFunding

Definition: The collective effort of individuals who network and pool their resources online to support efforts initiated by other people or organizations.

▪CrowdSourcing

Definition: A process that involves outsourcing tasks to a group of people online and offline.

○Crown Books

Crown Books (retail) is of no relation to Crown Books (publisher), although the former carried inventory from the latter. Crown Books (retail) went bankrupt in 2001. Andy Weiss, owner of a private bookseller called A&S Booksellers, bought the Crown Books name and applied the name and trademark to most of his stores. In 2007, Ward Albright purchased the right to share the name with Weiss and opened more retail outlets. Today, Crown Books buys remaindered books and overstock in bulk from publishers at large discounts and passes the savings to customers.

▪CTA

Call to Action (**CTA**) is an author's marketing technique usually placed in the back of the book. The strategy is considered a disappointment to most. The idea is to identify what else readers would want after reading. Sometimes the publisher would recommend one specific title that could help. In theory, this encourages readers to keep buying more books from the publisher.

◊Customer Reviews

Amazon allows consumers to voice their opinions. The default display appears below the book description and is in order from newest to oldest. On most detail pages, however, one or two "Spotlight Reviews" appear at the beginning of the customer reviews section. One can also sort customer reviews by different criteria. Spotlight Reviews and sorting criteria are based on how well the review was written and how helpful it was deemed. Displays on the site are arranged so that a prospective buyer can get good information quickly.

Anyone registered as an Amazon.com customer is entitled to write customer reviews. It doesn't matter where an item was purchased, or if it was a gift, or if the reviewer just borrowed it for a weekend. If someone feels moved to write a review, as a registered Amazon.com customer, they are welcome.

▪Cutline

Description: The cutline is also called a caption which is the legend or explanation that identifies an illustration or photograph.

▪CYMK

Description: The four colors used in printing that includes three primary colors; cyan, yellow, magenta, and black.

4 D-E

D

▪Daisy

Description: A global consortium of organizations that work to ensure that all published information is available to people with print disabilities, at the same time and at no greater cost, in an accessible, feature-rich, navigable format.

○Dalkey Archive Press

Dalkey Archive Press is a publisher of fiction, poetry, and literary criticism located in the United States, Dublin, and London. Their specialization is in the publication or republication of lesser known, often avant-garde works. The publisher is named for the novel The Dalkey Archive, by the Irish author Flann O'Brien. In 2011, the Press was awarded the Lifetime Achievement Award from the National Book Critics Circle; its authors and translators have been recipients of many major awards, including the Nobel Prize, the Independent Foreign Fiction Prize, the Helen and Kurt Wolff Translator's Prize, the Vondel Prize, and the Premio Valle-Inclán award.

▪Dash

Description: A punctuation method authors and editors use. A dash is used when dialogue is cut off or interrupted. The industry rule is to not add any other punctuation. Example: "It wasn't my-"

▪Database

Definition: Data stored and managed by a DBMS (database management system). The process can be as simple as a mailing list or as complex as necessary to provide data management for easy accessibility.

▪DBA

DBA stands for Doing Business As. The term is used when a name other than one's own is the business name.

▪Dedication

Definition: An inscription honoring the person(s) who inspired the work. The dedication is made part of the book's front matter.

▪Delete

Definition: A proofreading directive to remove certain characters or material.

○Delicious

Del.icio.us is a social bookmarking site where members can store, annotate, and share favorite Web pages.

▪Democratization

Definition: A fundamental change in publishing where anyone with a computer and a word-processor application can publish a book and anyone with a computer, tablet, or smart phone can buy a book.

▪Demographics

Definition: A profile of a group (readers, listeners, viewers, etc.) documenting such things as age, sex, marital status, education, socioeconomic level, and hobbies.

▪Density

Definition: The relative darkness of an image area. In photography, the blackening or light-stopping ability of a photographic image, as numerically measured by a densitometer.

▪Desktop Publishing

Desktop publishing is the production of printed material by way of a personal computer, laser printer, and publishing software.

▪Dialogue

Dialogue is sometimes spelled **dialog** in American English. Basically, it is a literary and theatrical form of expression consisting of a written or spoken conversational exchange between two or more parties. Historical origins refer to narrative, both philosophical or didactic devices, and found in classical Greek and Indian literature. Professional work formats dialogue correctly. Foundation principles generally are..

1. Every new speaker requires a new paragraph, even if the sentence is one word.

2. Avoid beginning a story with dialogue.

3. Learn and use proper punctuation.

○ Dictionary/Wikipedia Access

Description: An integrated linkage of dictionary and Wikipedia inside an ebook format that allows users to get clarification about words and items they may not fully comprehend.

▪ Die-Cut

Definition: The creation of openings, shapes, or folds by cutting away part of the paper stock.

○ Digg.com

Digg is a social news Web site where people share content by submitting links and stories, and then vote on them. The more popular the Web page, the higher its position on the site.

▪ Digital Printing

Definition: Printing technology linking printing presses to computers, resulting in rapid turnaround times and lower production costs. The method is frequently used for on-demand or short-run color printing.

◊ Digital Rights Management

Digital Rights Management (DRM) is a method not allowing book sharing. This particular option can't change once selected.

▪Direct Sales

Digital system where authors sell their ebooks or printed books directly to readers.

▪Dirty Copy

Definition: Heavily edited or marked up copy difficult to read.

◊Discussion Boards

Discussion Boards are a free service to enable readers, publishers, and authors the forum to share comments about material available on the Amazon site. This service is available only to individuals older than 13 years of age who have purchased items from Amazon.com and are in good standing in the Amazon.com community. Parties who use the Amazon.com discussion boards, are certifying that they are old enough to participate. To find discussion boards with Amazon.com customers who share common interests, go to *Customer Communities*.

▪Disintermediation

Definition: Cutting out intermediaries, such as publishers, distributors, wholesalers and bookstores. The idea that entities that do not add value to a process eventually get removed. Traditional publishers must fight disintermediation in a world where self-publishers can produce books of equal or better quality.

▪Display Ad

Definition: A print advertisement using graphics in the display.

▪Display Type

Definition: A type that is larger than the text, as in a chapter headline.

▪Distributor

A distributor is a company that acts like a source for book publishers, selling primarily to the book trade. Some companies provide exclusive distribution rights, may act as a wholesaler or a warehouse of publisher's titles. Many companies distribute other products, and some sell directly to the public (Amazon.com). Book distributors offer a consolidated list of publisher's titles, so that bookstores can purchase from a wider range of publishers than if they had to open separate accounts with each publisher, who often require a minimum order that the bookstore cannot meet. Most small or independent publishers have relations with a distributor, including self-published authors, who often use professional services to sell to the public. A few large publishing companies, including the "Big Six", also act as distributors for the numerous imprints they have acquired over the years.

▪Domain Name

Description: The unique name that identifies an Internet site.

◊DotCom Crash

Amazon.com survived the *dotcom* crash, but was hit hard. From a high of around $100, at one point its shares reached a low of just $6. In fact, Amazon.com saw losses of $3 billion in its early years and didn't report a profit until the last quarter of 2001 -- six years after launch. It didn't see full-year profit until 2003. Bezos, however, was not fazed by the drop. Fast Company reported on a presentation the Amazon.com founder made to a PC Forum conference in 2001. First, Bezos showed a slide focusing on Amazon's stock as it fell from its $100-a-share peak (adjusted for splits) to its $6 nadir. "If you look at things this way," he said, "you're a pessimist." Then he displayed a slide charting Amazon's cumulative wealth creation as a sharp upward line between two points: the day the stock went public ($1.50, split-adjusted) and that day ($11.64). "I prefer to look at it this way," Bezos told the tough crowd, "and that's why I'm an optimist."

Doubleday

Doubleday was founded in 1897, when Frank Nelson Doubleday formed Doubleday & McClure Company in partnership with magazine publisher Samuel McClure. Among their first bestsellers was _The Day's Work_ by Rudyard Kipling. Today, Doubleday and its Nan A. Talese imprint publish an array of commercial fiction, literary fiction and serious nonfiction titles. Among the bestselling and prize-winning authors published by Doubleday are Anne Applebaum, Pat Barker, Dan Brown, Bill Bryson, William D. Cohan, Barbara Delinsky, Sebastian Faulks, George Friedman, David Grann, John Grisham, Mark Haddon, Jon Krakauer, Jonathan Lethem, Jeff Lindsay, Christopher Reich, Rick Reilly, Edward Rutherfurd, Hampton Sides, Jeffrey Toobin, and Colson Whitehead. Nan A. Talese authors include Peter Ackroyd, Margaret Atwood, Thomas Cahill, Pat Conroy, Lady Antonia Fraser, Adam Haslett, Thomas Keneally, Valerie Martin and Ian McEwan.

▪Downtime

Definition: Time when a supplier is not busy and may give better prices. Also the time during which a given piece of equipment is inoperable and/or under repair.

▪DPI

DPI stands for dots per inch. The more dpi, the sharper the image reproduction. In printing, DPI (dots per inch) refers to the output resolution of a printer or image-setter, and PPI (pixels per inch) refers to the input resolution of a photograph or image

▪Dropbox

A dropbox is a modern online service letting users sync photos, videos, and documents to a cloud-based system while making the files available on multiple computers and devices.

▪Dumb apostrophe

Definition: An industry slang term that refers to an apostrophe that appears as a vertical stroke rather than an open or closed mark.

▪Dumb dash

Definition: An industry term used when an **em** dash appears as two hyphens or even as one hyphen in lieu of an en dash.

▪Dumb quotation marks

Definition: An industry term referencing quote marks as a couple of vertical strokes in lieu of the correct open or closed quotation marks.

▪Dumb Titles

Discussion: It's not easy to write book title. They should be snappy, say what the book's about, and usually all in two or three words. A great title is the secret to a fiction book's marketability.

▪Dummy

Definition: A preliminary mock-up of a book folded to the exact size of the finished work.

▪Dummy Folio

Definition: "Working" page numbers added for identification purposes is an example of dummy folio, but change before the final printed book.

▪Dump

Description: A display for books, usually made of cardboard; sometimes called a counter stand or floor stand (standee).

▪Duotone

Definition: The process for producing an illustration in two colors from a one color original that gives a quality of added depth and texture.

▪Dust Jacket

Description: A protective and attractive cover for hardback books that provides space for visual display and promotional copy, also called a dust cover, book cover, or jacket.

E

▪EAN

The EAN (European Article Number)is a 13 digit barcode used on retail products globally. All retail products feature a single standard EAN barcode. The exceptions to this rule are: books, magazines, and prescription drugs. EAN is the standard adopted by all countries worldwide, except for the U.S. and Canada.

▪Ebooks

An ebook is an electronic book. There are several mays to express this spelling or description: e-book, eBook, e-Book, ebook, digital book, or even e-edition. When the term first became popular, it stood for a book-length publication in digital form, consisting of text, images, or both, readable on computers or other electronic devices; more or less defined as an electronic version of a printed book. Today, many e-books exist without any printed equivalent. Commercially produced and sold, they are usually intended to be read on dedicated e-book readers, however, almost any sophisticated electronic device that features a controllable viewing screen, including computers, many mobile phones, and all smartphones can also be used to read e-books.

EBIDTA

EBIDTA stands for a publisher's Earnings Before Interest, Taxes, Depreciation, and Amortization. The term is an accounting metric computed by considering a company's earnings before interest payments, tax, depreciation, and amortization are subtracted for any final accounting of its income and expenses. The EBITDA of a business gives an indication of its current operational profitability, i.e., how much profit it makes with its present assets and its operations on the products it produces and sells.

Ebook reseller

The term describes reseller merchants who acquire rights from authors to sell ebooks and generally include major stores like Amazon (Kindle), Apple (iBookstore), Barnes & Noble (Nook), Google (Google Play), and Kobo.

EDI

EDI stands for Electronic Data Interchange. It enables the computer system from one company to "talk" to the computer system of another company and digitally exchange data. Because this digital exchange of data is facilitated using computers, most, if not all of the associated business processes can be automated so they occur with little or no manual data entry. This enables companies to electronically send and receive business documents like purchase orders and invoices using EDI transaction codes.

Selling a book on Amazon, one very popular option, is by short discounting through EDI. Various book wholesalers, which includes Ingram (has direct relationship with Amazon.com) requires a technical partnership with another publisher or distributor. On-Demand (POD) companies have an EDI relationship with Ingram, for example.

○ Edit911

Edit911.com is a website where authors can hire editors and proofreaders who are experts in editing services.

■ Edition

Generally, edition refers to all printed books from the same unaltered boards. Once a change is made, the book becomes a second edition and so-on.

■ Editor

Generally speaking, an editor is one who does **editing**; a procedure of selecting and preparing written, visual, audible, and film media used to convey information. Editors can go by various titles (especially true in large publishing companies), but the process generally involves correction, condensation, organization, and many other modifications performed with an intention of producing a correct, consistent, accurate and complete work. The editing process often begins with the author's idea for the work, continuing as collaboration as the work is created. As such, editing can involve creative skills, human relations and a precise set of methods.

▪Editor-in-Chief

Description: The top editorial executive in a publishing program, setting policy for that program and directing acquisitions.

▪E-Junkie

A website that is designed to help authors sell books directly and charges according to the number of files and storage space amount used, while download numbers are limited.

○Elance

Elance.com is a website where authors can locate industry related independent contractors.

▪Electronic Publishing

Electronic Publishing is a general term embracing all forms of computerized publication, particularly those that deliver text or other materials directly to the consumer's computer screen.

▪Elegy

An **elegy** is a sad, mournful or sorrowful poem, especially a funeral refrain or a lament for the dead. "Elegy" (sometimes spelled elégie) may also denote a type of musical work, usually of a somber nature.

▪Elhi Market

Definition: Elhi is an adjective that means elementary and high school students.

▪Ellipsis

Definition: A general punctuation used when dialogue fades away. Example: "I just..." She hugged. "I thought mom loved me."

○Elsevier

Elsevier is an academic publishing company which publishes medical and scientific literature. It is a part of the Reed Elsevier group. Based in Amsterdam, the company has operations in the United Kingdom, USA, Mexico, Brazil, Spain and elsewhere.

▪Email Newsletter

Description: A digital publication distributed via e-mail to inform readers about an author's current ventures.

▪Em dash

Definition: A general punctuation dash the width of the letter "m". The nomenclature replaces commas, semicolons, and parentheses for emphasis, an interruption, or abrupt thought change.

▪Embossing

Description: Raising the image above the paper level, such as a title on the book cover.

▪Encryption

Definition: An encoding information process for security purposes.

En dash

Definition: A general punctuation dash that indicates a closed range of values such as dates, times, and numbers. In some cases it acts as a hyphen connecting adjectives or prefixes to open compounds.

Endpapers

Definition: An industry term referring to the heavy sheets that fasten the pages of a hardcover book to the cover.

Engraving

Description: The cutting of a design into a block of material, resulting in a pattern from which a print can be made.

Enlargement

Description: The photographic process of creating an image larger than the original.

Epic

An **epic** is any work of literature, film, etc., having heroic deeds for its subject matter or having other qualities associated with the epic: like a Hollywood epic. Traditionally it relates to a classification of poetry, known as epic poetry. However in modern terms, epic is often extended to other art forms, such as epic theatre, films, music, novels, plays, television shows, and video games, wherein the story has a theme of grandeur and heroism.

▪Epigraph

Definition: A phrase, quotation, or poem placed at the book's beginning or start of a chapter.

▪Epilogue

Definition: A concluding section that rounds out a story and often updates the reader. Part of the text, not the back matter.

▪EPS

Encapsulated PostScript (EPS) is a DSC-conforming PostScript document with additional restrictions which is intended to be usable as a graphics file format. In other words, EPS files are more-or-less self-contained, reasonably predictable PostScript documents that describe an image or drawing and can be placed within another PostScript document. Simply, an EPS file is a PostScript program, saved as a single file that includes a low-resolution preview "encapsulated" inside of it, allowing some programs to display a preview on the screen.

▪EPUB

The file format name is for an ebook that's used by most online resellers and ebook readers (except Amazon and Kindle), based on a ZIP archive and HTML files.

○EPUB check

EPUB files (formatted to EPUB standard file extension ".epub) are validated using this valuable tool. Version 2.0 and later versions detect many types of errors in EPUB formatted files.

○EPUB conversion site

A website designed to transform a Microsoft Word document into an EPUB file. This allows a user to preview an actual Kindle or Nook book before uploading to a major ebook reseller.

▪EReaders

A slang industry term referencing any device designed for reading ebooks.

○Ereader News Today

Ereadernewstoday.com offers free books, tips, and tricks for Kindle readers. This is an excellent starting place for self-publishing. Authors can pitch their book to bloggers and reviewers at the beginning of a marketing campaign.

▪Errata

Description: A loose sheet listing errors found inside the printed book. Commonly corrected, prior to the book's next printing, by the insertion of a loose sheet called an errata sheet consisting of revised text in each copy of the book.

▪Espresso Book Machines

Description: A self-contained unit that prints and binds softcover books. The assembly is a print on demand (POD) machine that prints, collates, covers, and binds a single book in a few minutes. The **EBM** is small enough to fit in a retail book store or small library room and can potentially allow readers to obtain any book title, even books that are out of print. The machine uses a PDF file and prints, binds, and trims the reader's selection as a paperback book.

▪Evergreen

Description: A book or article that is timeless.

○Everyman's Library

Everyman's Library was founded on February 15, 1906 with the publication by Joseph Dent (1849-1926) of fifty titles. Dent, a master London bookbinder turned publisher, was a classic Victorian autodidact. The tenth child of a Darlington housepainter, he had left school at thirteen, and arrived in London with half-a-crown in his pocket. Dent promised to publish new and beautiful editions of the world's classics at one shilling a volume.

▪Excerpt

Definition: A portion taken from a longer work, also called an extract.

▪Exclusive

Description: A publisher's reference to a news or feature story printed by one media source substantially ahead of competition. Usually there's sole distribution rights to specific markets for works given to a distributor.

▪Expert Read

Generally, this means a reading of a book by the book's authority figure who determines the accuracy and completeness prior to publication, which is sometimes called a peer read.

▪Ezine

Definition: A general slang term meaning an electronic magazine available on line.

5 F-G

F

▪FaberNovel

FaberNovel is an international innovation agency founded in 2003, with offices in Paris, San Francisco, New York, Moscow, and Lisbon. The agency conceives, designs, and executes digital initiatives for large companies, organizations and government agencies. FaberNovel is known as ideas with legs. Their most popular study, completed in 2011, was about "The Hidden Empire" which was all about Amazon's strategies for dominating online retail. Currently, the research has been updated to include analyses on all of the company's latest moves, and insights into where they may be going next.

○Facebook

Facebook.com is a popular social-media website with more than one billion users. Popular with authors, personal profiles are created. Status updates, reports, and photos can easily be exchanged using the "friends" exchange messages.

▪Facing Page

Description: Any page that forms a double spread with another.

▪Fair Use

A legal term making allowable a limited amount of copyrighted material without permission granted.

▪FAQ

FAQ stands for Frequently Asked Questions. Documents sometimes list answers to the common questions on a particular subject matter or problem area. This is a frequently used Internet term. It is used frequently on tabs, toggles, and buttons where this label opens a document that lists answers to most common questions on a particular subject or problem area.

▪F&G's

A slang expression that simply means folded and gathered pages. The unbound signatures of a book sometimes are sent to reviewers.

◊FBA

Fulfillment by Amazon (**FBA**) is a service allowing one to generate profits from a minimal amount of effort and launch a business from home. ScoutBotPro.com; is software allowing one to buy inventory online at highly profitable prices. BookSalesFound.com; keeps one up to date on area book sales. listtee.com expedites a tedious listing process, saves time and money and is a great tool for buying money-making inventory in the field. Sell it and Amazon ships it. Leverage Amazon's fulfillment networks and expertise so customers and one's business benefits. Send products to fulfillment centers, and Amazon will pack and ship them and provide customer service. Fulfillments are also eligible for free shipping on orders over $35 and Amazon Prime; other delivery options are available for competitive pricing. **FBA** listings on Amazon.com are sorted by product price and listings are displayed with the "Fulfillment by Amazon" logo, so customers know that packing, delivery, customer service, and returns are all handled by Amazon. **FBA** can also fulfill orders from other sales channels using inventory stored at an Amazon fulfillment center. The seller can manage inventory through a simple online user interface that can direct or return the inventory at any time. Customers also benefit from a growing assortment of other benefits, such as gift wrapping and an up-to-the-minute countdown for One Day Shipping.

▪Field

Field, as used in the publishing industry, is a structured place of social positions which can be occupied by agents and organizations. The position of agents or organizations depends on the type and quantity of resources or capital available. Any social arena or business sector can be treated as a field as well as a sphere of education or a sport domain. Within this theater the agents and organizations are linked together in relations of cooperation, competition and interdependency. The book market is an important field but generally, it really is more than markets. They too are made up of agents and organizations, all of different kinds and quantities of power and resources. It is a field with a variety of practices, specific forms of competition, collaboration and reward. Four distinct aspects help define the publishing world.

1. Publishing is not one world, it's a plurality of fields each with its own characteristics.

2. Agents and organizations are always one part of a whole, like a system.

3. Power is the capacity to act and get things done and depends on resources and capital.

4. Logic of the Field, factors (like language) determine conditions in which agents participate.

▪Filler

An author or publisher's slang; basically, the term is used for referencing useless wording to pad a book's word count.

▪First Edition

The entire original printing from the same plates (unchanged).

◊First Sale

Amazon.com sold its first book from Jeff Bezos' Seattle area garage in July of 1995. The book was Fluid Concepts & Creative Analogies: Computer Models of the Fundamental Mechanisms of Thought. During its first month in business, Amazon.com received orders from people in 50 U.S. states and 45 countries across the world.

▪First Serial Rights

The exclusive right to serialize a book in a periodical.

○ **Fiverr**

A website offering a variety of *pay-for* contract services.

■ **Flap Copy**

Definition: The material describing a book and its author that appears on the inside folds of the dust jacket.

■ **Flat**

Description: An industry printing term describing the assembling of negatives on a heavy paper sheet for platemaking (see stripping).

■ **Flat Fee**

Definition: A onetime payment for a job or task, such as the preparation of text or artwork.

■ **Flier**

Description: An inexpensive promotional piece often printed on 8 ½ x 11 paper.

■ **Flop**

Definition: To flip over a photograph negative so the image is reversed.

Flush

Definition: To be even with, such as in "flush right," or "flush left."

Flyer

Definition: A printed announcement. A flyer becomes a brochure when folded.

FOB

An abbreviation that stands for Free On Board. _FOB origin_ means the addressee pays the shipping. _FOB Los Angeles_ means the goods are delivered free as far as Los Angeles, then the addressee pays for transport, if any, from there.

Foil

Definition: A hot stamping shiny material normally found on the front cover of a book. It can be gold, silver, or standard colors, such as red, blue, green, etc.

Folio

Definition: The number character on the book page is called a folio.

Font

Definition: The complete set of type that's in a single typeface, including characters, numbers and punctuation marks.

▪Footnote

Definition: A reference, explanation, or comment placed below the text on a page.

▪Foreign Rights

Description: Rights for publishing a book in a foreign country are negotiated. Foreign rights are usually sold by an author's publisher to other publishers in different countries. As a self-publisher, the author can publish in the native language worldwide and maintain foreign rights. But, selling rights to a foreign publisher often involves the foreign publisher translating the work to the local language as well.

▪Forecasting

Definition: The means of using mathematical computations to predict business trends.

▪Foreword

Definition: prefatory words by someone other than the author.

▪Format

Definition: Designation of typeface, margins, boxing, or any other special treatment of copy. The term is also used referencing the trim size and physical book layout.

▪Formatting

Definition: The process of designing a publication.

▪Forum

Definition: Another name for a newsgroup or chat room.

◊Four Degrees

Amazon.com has four levels or degrees of program selling.

1. **Individual Selling Account.** Applies to all with an Amazon Consumer Account, click on the SELL YOURS HERE button on any product page. No listing fees apply, in this case. Offer to sell a used or new book and Amazon collects 15 percent commission plus additional miscellaneous charges.

2. **Pro-Merchant Subscribers.** Amazon.com charges a monthly fee ($39.99 or more) which allows multiple listings and management assistance. The advantage for this program is the elimination of the standard single item fee charged to individual accounts. This service makes sense for sales of more than 40 items each month.

3. **Fulfillment by Amazon.com.** Sellers ship items direct to Amazon's warehouse, in this case. The big advantage for independent sellers is that extra fees now include merchandise storage, customer service, and shipping. This option also qualifies for Amazon's free shipping offers.

4. **Merchants@ Program.** This service exceeds the Pro-Merchant status, sometimes called Gold & Platinum Level. Participants are generally large-volume vendors with access to wholesale prices. Invitations for this service are granted to existing Pro-Merchant Subscribers.

◊FPS

Amazon.com has a Flexible Payment Service (**FPS**) module available to web site developers. A customized payment process, when installed, makes every transaction go through with hands-off technology. http://www.amazon.com/b?ie=UTF8&node=34240011

▪Freelancer

Definition: Skilled creative people such as writers, editors, graphic artists, consultants, etc. who sell services as independent contractors.

▪Freemium

A business model where a book is provided free of charge. But, there's a premium assessed for advanced features, functionality, or virtual items.

▪Front & Back List

Front-list books are the new titles in the marketplace; back-list books are the books that have been available for a while. When marketing a book—your own or someone else's—understand how book marketing strategy is different for front-list and back-list titles. Building a strong backlist has traditionally been seen as the way to produce a profitable publishing house. That's because the most expensive aspects of the publishing process would be paid for and the only remaining expenses are reproduction costs and author royalty. A strong backlist is also a form of The Long Tail in modern business plans.

▪Front Flap

The front, inside flap of a dust jacket covering a hardcover book.

▪Front Matter

All books have front pages which are called front matter, similar to a sandwich which has a piece of bread on the top and bottom to hold the ingredients inside. Traditionally, the front matter consists of four distinct areas. Page A is the half-title (also called the bastard title) page consisting only of the main title. Page B is the verso which is the back of the half-title and is usually left blank. Page C is the second page on the right (recto) which is the full title page. It includes the title, subtitle, author's name, and publisher. Also included would be the illustrator's, editor's, photographers, and the forward writer's name if famous. Page D is the copyright page (title page verso – back of the title page). Normally, full information is presented. Page E is a good location for the book's dedication or acknowledgement. Also, a list of other books by the author can be placed here. Page F is generally the forward or note to the reader or preface. Page G is the table of contents and begins on the recto page.

▪Frontispiece

A decorative illustration that appears in the front matter of a book, usually facing the title page. Also called front plate.

▪FTP File Transfer Protocol

A standard method of sending files between computers over the internet. FTP is built on a client-server architecture and uses separate control and data connections between the client and the server. FTP users may authenticate themselves using a clear-text sign-in protocol, normally in the form of a username and password, but can connect anonymously if the server is configured to allow it. For secure transmission that encrypts the username, password, and content, FTP is often secured with SSL/TLS ("FTPS").

Fulfillment

The process of ordering, picking, packing, filling and shipping of book orders.

G

○ Gale

Gale, (Founded in Detroit in 1954 by Frederick Gale Ruffner, it was acquired by Thomson in 1985) is an educational publishing company based in Farmington Hills, Michigan, in the western suburbs of Detroit. It was part of the Thomson Learning division of the Thomson Corporation, a Canadian company, but became part of Cengage Learning in 2007. The company, formerly known as Gale Research and the Gale Group, is active in research and educational publishing for public and academic libraries, schools and businesses. The company may be best known for its full-text magazine and newspaper database, InfoTrac, and other online databases accessible from schools and libraries, as well as multi-volume reference works, especially in the areas of religion, history and social science.

■ Galley

Originally, the term was used for proof sheets run on the press to check the typesetting. Later, the typeset pages prior to paste-up was called galley. Today, prepublication copies sent out for review are galleys. They are proofs issued in the proofreading and copy-editing review phase sometimes called galley proofs.

▪Gang Run

Sometimes called ganging, the term refers to putting numerous unrelated jobs together for printing. This provides lower costs by economizing setup charges.

○Ganxy

Ganxy.com is a website that enables authors to sell ebooks directly to readers.

▪Gate Keeper

Description: An editor or other person responsible for decisions on what will be published, and how a company's list will develop. A customer or fund-holder who determines what will be authorized for adoption or expenditure, typically in an educational institution.

○Gebbie Press

The Gebbie Press offers three ways to contact the media. Just ONE well-placed press release can generate tremendous interest in new titles. Every day editors set aside space for press releases. They offer three ways to distribute releases and to contact the media. (http://www.gebbieinc.com)

> 1. **PRPro**, the turnkey online press release distribution service which is constantly updated, creating a media contact list and press release distribution.

2. The **All-In-One Media Directory** - print version.
A compact yet comprehensive 8 1/2 x 11 reference work detailing media contact information for more than 24,000 media outlets in one place.

3. Excel and .csv data only file formats that are constantly updated. Media contact database easily imports into a database, mailing list, contact manager, fax, email, spreadsheet or other program.

○**GDPBM**

The Gale Directory of Publications and Broadcast Media (GDPBM) is a four-volume set revised annually and indexed by state. It includes regional markets, networks, and syndicates. Published by Gale, this premier media directory contains thousands of listings for radio and television stations and cable companies. Print media entries provide address; phone, fax numbers, and e-mail address; key personnel, including feature editors; and much more. Broadcast media entries provide address; phone, fax, and e-mail addresses; key personnel; owner information; hours of operation; networks carried and more.

▪**Genre**

Definition: A category of specific kind of writing, such as historical, science fiction, or mystery.

▪**Ghostwriter**

A ghostwriter is a professional writer who produces books, stories, or any other form of texts attributed to others.

▪GIF Graphics Interchange Format

Description: A file format commonly used to display graphics and images in HTML documents on the Internet.

▪Global Distribution

Description: The process of making a publication available for purchase in many countries worldwide. For example, Kindle Direct Publishing lists an ebook in one hundred countries and iBook stores in fifty countries.

▪Glossary

Definition: A list of items in alphabetical order located at the end of a book that includes relevant and important items.

▪Glossy

Description: A photograph with a shiny surface as opposed to matte.

◊Gift

Amazon.com offers a couple of gifting options. 1. Send as Gift: Buy a book and deliver it to friend. Click the button on a book's page. 2. Gift Card: (as low as $1.00) can be sent to someone to spend on Amazon.

◊GoodReads

Amazon Trademark; the popular social service that allows users to share what they are reading with friends. The website recently made it a lot easier for users to add new purchases from Amazon to their bookshelves. Many people make book purchases from Amazon, son this was a smart move for the social reading service. The new feature is quite easy to use, with a simple link from the "My Books" page that allows users to add physical book purchases and Kindle purchases to their library. From there, users simply logs-in with appropriate Amazon credentials, then rates the books they've purchased, and adds them to the targeted shelf to show off to their friends.

The only surprising thing about this move is how long it took, seeing as Amazon purchased *Goodreads* well over a year ago. It seems like this integration would have been one of the first items on Amazon's to-do list, as merging the two services makes a better experience for users while also incentivizing users to buy from Amazon for easier access to managing their library.

○Google AdWords keyword tool

One type of website where users can enter keywords to find out how many times each month that people search those particular terms on Google.

○Google Docs

This cloud-based word processor is very useful for sharing an outline or a portion of a book.

○**Google+ / Google+Blog**

Google+ is a social network. The Blog WordPress pluging enables posts to become a WordPress blog post. The Google+community is also a feature that enables people to form public and private groups to share interests.

■**Gothic Novel**

A slang description sometimes referred to as Gothic fiction or Gothic horror, which is a genre or mode of literature that combines elements of both horror and romance that ultimately feeds on a pleasing sort of terror. Interestingly, Gothic literature is closely associated with the Gothic Revival of architecture more or less in the same era. In a similar fashion to the Gothic revivalists' dismissal of the precision and rationalism of the neoclassical style of the *Enlightened Establishment*, literary Gothic exemplifies an appreciation of the joys of extreme emotion, the thrills of fearfulness, and the unique awe that might be inherent in the sublime quest for atmosphere. At least that's the way it was until Edgar Allan Poe reinterpreted Gothic fiction.

■**Graphics**

The illustrative and decorative elements in a work.

■**Gripper Margin**

The unprintable edge of the sheet of paper where the printing press or photocopier clamps the sheet to pull it through the printing machine; often on top of the sheet and usually 0.25 inches.

○GSWC

The abbreviation stands for Get Started Write Challenge, an annual event sponsored by Writersmarket.com.

◊Guidelines

Guidelines are terms and agreements applicable to that Amazon Service ("Service Terms"). If these Conditions of Use are inconsistent with the Service Terms, those Service Terms will control.

■Guideposts

Elements of a book that writers use to assist readers to work their way through the text.

○Gumroad

This website enables authors to sell ebooks directly to readers.

■Gutter

The space between columns of type, such as the inner margins in two facing pages of a book.

6 H-I-J

H

▪Hairline

Definition: A very finely ruled line in printing.

◊Hall of Fame Reviewer

The Amazon's Top 50 Reviewer List has someone that is given the Hall-of-Fame title when they rise to the 10th ranking, or better.

▪Half Title

Description: Sometimes called bastard title, it is best described as a page on which the book title stands alone and precedes the complete title page.

▪Halftone

Description: A screened photograph. A tone pattern composed of dots of uniform density but varying in size. A reproduction of a photo whereby the various tones (highlights and shadows) are translated into numerous tiny dots for printing.

▪Halftone Screen

Description: A screen placed in front of the negative material in the process camera to break up a continuous tone image into dots of black and white to produce a halftone. There are two types: ruled glass screens and contact screens.

○Hangouts on Air

Description: This Google+ feature enables groups of up to ten to create live broadcasts that can be viewed publicly.

▪Hardcover

Description: A book that is bound with unbending protective covers that may also have a flexible sewn spine (case bound).

▪Hash Tags

Definition: A symbol that is used to mark keywords or topics (#). Doing this will help people find subjects easier and is searchable to most search engines. Example: #cupcake recipes. The hashtag symbol in this description, can be clicked on to instantly search through (like photos that relate to cupcakes).

▪Headband

Definition: Reinforcing cloth at each end of the spine of a hardcover book.

▪Hexameter

A **Hexameter** is a rhythmical unit pattern of language (poems or plays). Since the word begins with HEX, it is metrical, meaning it pertains to poetic measures of a verse consisting of six feet, which refers to the basic unit that generates a line of verse. The unit is composed of syllables, the number of which is limited, with a few variations, by the sound pattern the foot represents.

○Hibari

Hibari is a standalone software application for Twitter featuring a one-column orientation.

▪Hickey

Definition: A slang term referencing a speck or blotch on a printed page.

▪Highlighting

Definition: A particular feature incorporated into some ebook reading applications that allow readers to mark important text.

○Hootsuite

A social media tool that acts as a hub in managing social-media efforts across multiple platforms including Google+, Facebook, and Twitter.

○ Houghton Mifflin Harcourt

Houghton Mifflin Harcourt is an educational and trade publisher headquartered in Boston's Back Bay. It publishes textbooks, instructional technology materials, assessments, reference works, and fiction and non-fiction for both young readers and adults.

▪House Organ

Definition: A periodical or newsletter issued by a firm or organization for its members, employers, customers, or prospects.

▪HTML – Hyper Text Markup Language

Definition: A coding language used to create documents for use on the World Wide Web. **HTML** is written in the form of special elements consisting of tags enclosed in angle brackets. Tags commonly come in pairs like <b1> and </b1>, although some tags represent empty components and unpaired, for example <img>. The first in a pair is the start tag, and the second is the end tag. They are also called opening tags and closing tags. There are hundreds of HTML tutorials websites like;

www.htmlgoodies.com or www.w3schools.com

where anyone can learn the basics. The purpose of a web browser is to read HTML documents and compose them into visible or audible web pages. The browser does not display the HTML tags, but uses the tags to interpret the content of the page. HTML describes the structure of a website semantically along with cues for presentation, making it a markup language rather than a programming language.

HTML elements form the building blocks of all websites and allows images and objects to be embedded used to create interactive forms. It provides a means to create structured documents by denoting structural semantics for text such as headings, paragraphs, lists, links, quotes and other items. It can embed scripts written in languages such as JavaScript which affect the behavior of HTML web pages.

▪Hyperbole

Definition: Exaggerated claims intended to sell a product or promote a person, also called hype.

▪Hyperlink

Definition: A link from a hypertext file or document to another location or file, typically activated by clicking on a highlighted word or image on the screen.

I

○I.A.B. The Interactive Advertising Bureau

IAB is comprised of more than 500 leading media and technology companies responsible for selling 86% of online advertising in the U.S. http://www.iab.net/

○iBooks Author

iBooks is a software application that authors can use to create Muti-Touch ebooks for iPads.

○iBookstore

Apple's platform to sell traditional ebooks as well as Muti-Touch ebooks.

○IBPA

Independent Book Publishers Association (**IBPA**) is a nonprofit trade group organization that specializes in co-op mailings and other marketing programs (formerly PMA – Publishers Marketing Association).

▪IDs

Independent Distributor Wholesalers are also known as jobbers. They buy books and magazines in large amounts for resale to non-bookstore retail outlets such as newsstands, grocery stores, drug stores, hotels and airport shops.

▪Illustrations

Definition: Visual material such as photos, drawings, graphs, and tables.

▪Image Area

Definition: The printable area of a page where an image has been, or will be, produced.

▪Imposition

Definition: The positioning of pages for large press sheets so when cutting and folding is complete the images will be in the correct sequence.

▪Imprint

In the publishing industry, an imprint can mean several different things:

1. A piece of bibliographic information about a book, referencing the name, address of the book's publisher, and its date of publication as given at the foot or on the verso of its title page.

2. It can mean a trade name under which a work is published. For example, a publishing company may have multiple imprints; the different ones are used to market works to different demographics. In some cases, the diversity results from the takeover of smaller publishers (or parts of their business) by a larger company. Usage of the word has evolved and typically with a defining character or mission. Another example would be

the objective of Viking, being an imprint of The Penguin Group, "To publish a strictly limited list of good nonfiction, such as biography, history and works on contemporary affairs, and distinguished fiction with some claim to permanent importance rather than ephemeral popular interest." So, in effect, a publisher may have several imprints.

3. Finally, it can also refer to a finer distinction of a book's version. This is used to distinguish, for example different printings, or printing runs of the same edition, or to distinguish the same edition produced by a different publisher or printer. With the creation of the "ISBN" identification system, which is assigned to a text prior to its printing, a different imprint has effectively come to mean a text with a different ISBN—if one had been assigned to it.

◊Improve Your Recommendations

You can refine your recommendations by rating items or adjusting your collection ratings. To rate or update a product rating: Go to Improve Your Recommendations or click Fix this, which is next to recommended items on most items. Then, do the following to rate or update a specific rating.

1. Choose a rating of 1-5 stars or chose to leave the product unrated. The ratings you submit are private and are never shared with other Amazon.com customers, nor does it affect the average customer review for the item. These ratings are used solely by our recommendations service to provide you the most accurate recommendations possible.

2. To exclude certain purchases from being considered in your Recommendations:

3. Select Don't use for recommendations next to the purchased item or select This was a gift.

◊Immersion Reading

Immersion Reading allows yourself to become *Immersed* while in a story by narrating and highlighting the text as you read. This is available for those who own a Kindle Fire HD. You can read and listen simultaneously with real-time highlighting. It sparks an extra connection that boosts engagement, comprehension and retention, taking you deeper into the book.

▪Independent Contractor

Description: Generally, a person who is not considered an employee but privately hired to perform a specific task on a specific project is an independent contractor. An example is a copyeditor, a cover designer, or interior designer.

▪Independent Sellers

Generally, this industry term refers to a local general single-store book business. Independent sellers place their orders through a publisher's sales rep, who comes to the store, or through a publisher's telemarketing representative or wholesaler. Whereas a chain store receives books through store headquarters. But not all independent booksellers see reps so they rely on trade reviews and other sources of book news to decide which ones to order.

▪Index

An alphabetical record placed at the end of a book containing the names or subjects with references to the pages where they appear. It is an A to Z listing in the back matter giving the location of specific book content material.

▪India Ink

Description: The expression refers to dense jet black drawing ink for artwork.

○IndieBound

Independent bookseller members of the American Booksellers Association started this community-oriented movement. The idea is to bring together booksellers and readers who very much believe that a healthy economy relies on local sales which significantly help communities grow.

It's a powerful tool for **booksellers** to communicate their part in a national movement supporting independents--and lets everyone know just how many independent bookstores there are. It's powerful for **authors** to show their dedication to *indies* nationwide, easily done through linking to thousands of indie bookstores through IndieBound.org. It's powerful because *IndieBound* encompasses and supports **all types of independent retailers**, not just booksellers--and local or regional shop local campaigns and independent business alliances, as well. And it's powerful for **consumers** to feel a part of a larger movement, to know that their choices make a difference and that others are working toward the same goals.

○IndieReader Discovery Awards

Awards given to new indie writers by a panel of accredited reviewers; sponsored by IndieReader.com.

InfoTrac

InfoTrac is a program of complex text databases. It essentially uses content from academic journals and magazines, of which the majority are targeted to the English-speaking North American market. As is typical of databases, several forms of verification are used to confirm relationships with subscribing academic, public, and school libraries. InfoTrac databases are published by Gale, a part of Cengage Learning. In the late 1980s, InfoTrac was originally published on CD-ROMs which were mailed to subscribing libraries at regular intervals. During that time, when personal computers were still relatively new, many publishers were not yet licensing full text of their articles, so most publications were represented only by abstractions. Upgraded databases were published in coordination with various microfilm products which came about with sequentially numbered easy-loading cartridges. Then individual frames were individually numbered. Most extracts and full-text articles from the 1980s and 1990s have a code at the end of the article which points to the exact frame on a microfilm cartridge where the story begins, which a library user could use to obtain a copy of the article as originally published. Like most database companies, Gale started offering real-time access to these databases through a Web interface in the late 1990s (while simultaneously improving its full text coverage). Around 2000, Gale began making scanned articles in PDF format directly available through the Web interface. The InfoTrac brand was subsequently launched in 2005 on a new technology platform named Thomson Gale PowerSearch, named the "most improved product" at the 2005 Charleston Conference.

○ Ingram

Ingram is a book distribution company that got their start in 1964 as a textbook depository and have since grown and transformed into a comprehensive publishing industry services company that offers numerous solutions, including physical book distribution, print-on-demand and digital services. They work with over 30,000 publishers of all sizes around the world, either directly or indirectly. Ingram Content Group is the service provider to the book-publishing world; a distributor of content to retailers, libraries, schools, and other partners.

■ In-House

Definition: Those functions performed within a publishing company rather than by independent contractors. Also used to indicate that the finished books have been delivered to the publisher.

■ Input format

Input format is the starting file format used when converting from one format to another. One example is a Word DOC file conversion to an EPUB file. The input format is a Word DOC file.

■ Insert

Definition: Additional material added to a manuscript or book by an author or editor.

■ Insertion Order

Description: A form that is used by advertising agencies to place advertising in various media.

▪Interactive PDF

Description: Generally, a pdf file intended to be distributed as a digital book. Common characteristics of an interactive pdf includes hyperlink text underlined and colored to distinguish it from the surrounding text and a table of contents cross-linked to chapters and sections in the pdf.

○Interweb

Description: A sarcastic term for the internet. Often used in the context of parody regarding an inexperience, unskilled, or incoherent user. One important example is how some have trouble remembering but are required to use their password and username for one of several online accounts. But something happens called a *cookie*. Users notice while searching the web for "travel deals", for example, they suddenly start seeing travel display banners on other websites. Those ads are appearing because they've been *cookied*. In affiliate marketing, one task that *cookies* manage well is to remember the link or ad the visitor to a website clicks on. *Cookies* also have the capacity to store the date and time of the click, they can even be used to remember what kind of websites or content you like most. There are many different types of web *cookies* and uses, but the kind of cookie affiliate marketing relies on is called a first-party cookie. When a user visits a publisher's website and clicks an advertiser's creative ad, the visitor's browser receives the **CJ** tracking *cookie* that identifies the advertiser, the publisher, the specific creative and commission amount. This data is stored within the link information in what are called "parameters" and can include even more anonymous data used for attribution.

▪Inventory

Definition: Books on hand available for sale.

▪Invoice

Definition: A billing statement sent with a book order.

○iPod

A portable digital media player (MP3 player) and storage device manufactured by Apple Computer.

▪ISBN

ISBN stands for International Standard Book Number which is an essential identification number for ordering and cataloging purposes. An ISBN is required to list a new book for retail sale on Amazon.com. It can be found above the barcode on the back cover. In 2007, the 10-digit code was expanded to 13. The ISBN-13 is also called a Bookland EAN and is a subset of the EAN system. ISBN is the standard way of identifying book titles and separating them not only from each other, but also from their various publication formats, such as multiple editions, hardcover, paperback, audiocassette, CD-ROM, and so on. To apply contact: International Standard Book Numbering Agency R. R. Bowker 630 Central Avenue New Providence, NJ 07974 Telephone: (877) 310-7333 Fax: (908) 665-2895 http://www.isbn.org The process usually takes up to 10 business days.

▪ISP

ISP stands for Internet Service Provider which is a company that facilitates access to the Internet, usually at a cost to the consumer, although there are still some free community networks.

▪ISSN

ISSN stands for International Standard Serial Number which is similar to an ISBN but for serials or books published in a series. ISSNs are assigned by the Library of Congress.

▪Italics

Type with a right-hand slant and used for quotations, titles and emphasis.

○ⅠUniverse

iUniverse is a self-publishing company founded in October 1999 that publishes more than 5,000 new titles annually. The publisher is a pay-for-service company that has five different packages to choose from; Select, Premier, Premier Pro, Bookstore, and Book Launch.

J

Jacket

A jacket is sometimes called a book jacket, dust wrapper or dust cover. It is best described as the detachable outer cover, usually made of paper and printed with text and illustrations. This outer wrapper has folded flaps that hold it to the front and back of the hard cover book. Often the back panel or flaps are printed with biographical information about the author, a summary of the book from the publisher and sometimes quotable praises from celebrities or authorities in the book's subject area. In addition to its promotional role, the jacket protects the book covers from damage. Though itself relatively fragile, dust jackets have practical, aesthetic, and sometimes financial value. Sometimes the jacket may in turn be wrapped in another jacket, usually transparent, especially if the book is a library volume.

Job Printer

Description: One who buys books in large quantities for resale to retailers and libraries. A rack-jobber supplies books and magazines to racks in retail outlets.

Jobber

Definition: Basically a wholesale representative.

○JPEG

JPEG is a file extension that stands for *Joint Photographic Experts Group*. The format is commonly used to display graphics and images in HTML documents on the internet.

◇JustBooks

Amazon Trademark - BookFinder.com started operating in Europe under the JustBooks brand in 2006. There are currently JustBooks/BookFinder.com portals for the UK, France, Germany, and the Netherlands. Among the books from sellers whose inventories are indexed, users can find the lowest price for a book of their choice from over 125 million volumes available for sale, and purchase titles directly from the bookseller, without a markup. The search engine is focused primarily on English, French, German, Italian, Spanish, and Dutch language titles.

■Justification

Description: Composing lines of running text so that the left and right margins are even and automatically performed by computerized typesetting machines.

7 K-L

K

◊KDP

Kindle Direct Publishing makes it fast and easy to independently publish a book to the Kindle, for free. Plus, authors earn up to 70% royalties.

◊KDP Select

KDP Select is an optional program to reach more readers and opens the opportunity to earn more money. Choose to make a book exclusive to the Kindle Store, which is a requirement during a book's enrollment in KDP Select. Then the book becomes eligible to be included in the Kindle Owners' Lending Library (KOLL). This program offers free promotions for your own book for up to five days. Click the promotion Manager to see how many promotion days are used. Free offer is for up to 5 days each 90 day enrollment period. You can choose to do the full 5-day promotion right away, or space out promotion (3 days now, 2 days later). You'll want to set the date for free promotion to start 7 days from initiation because you should submit book to a few websites that will promote book on their website and they require at least 7 days' notice. Created for "Amazon Prime" members. If your book is enrolled, you make money every-time someone borrows your book. You also get the ability to promote book for free but are unable to publish anywhere else on internet. It becomes exclusive to Amazon and Kindle for those 90 days. Amazon Prime: a membership club where members pay a fee and get access to certain perks, one being able to "borrow" a book for free every month.

◊KDP Select Global Fund

The KDP Select global fund amount is $1.2 million for April 2014. We'll share the average global fund payout for March by the middle of April. In addition, KDP Select royalty information for March will be available on royalty reports in mid- April. Remember, if enrolled in KDP Select, you will earn a share of the global fund amount every time your book is borrowed from the Kindle Owners' Lending Library on Amazon.com, Amazon.co.uk, Amazon.de, Amazon.fr and Amazon.co.jp. Visit your Bookshelf to enroll your books in KDP Select.

◊KDP Community

Authors who join the Amazon KDP (Direct Publishing) Community take advantage of hosted Forums, which are a great place to learn from others and share industry experiences about independent publishing. Go to...

https://kdp.amazon.com/community/index.jspa The goal of the Kindle Direct Publishing Community is to provide an environment where members, no matter how new or experienced, can freely exchange thoughts, ideas, knowledge, and opinions. The Community is a dedicated support tool, and we place tremendous value on the information exchanged. Users of these forums are expected to follow the guidelines that are in place across other Amazon websites, including Amazon.com.

◊KDP Select

A Kindle Direct Publishing marketing program in which, in exchange for selling exclusively through Amazon, self-published authors can offer books for free for up to five days, put them in the Kindle Owners' Lending Library, access promotional opportunities, and share in a pool of money distributed to authors based on how many people borrow their book.

▪Kerning

Definition: Removing space between letters.

▪Key

Definition: An identifying explanation of coded material, such as a color-coded map and its accompanying key indicating what each color stands for.

▪Keyboarding

Definition: Entering data into a computer as opposed to typing a manuscript.

▪Keyline

Definition: Essentially the same as paste-up which is the original composite art for offset printing.

▪Keywords

Definition: Targeted words that allows an author or publisher to get more exposure by getting in front of searchers in a specific market. The objective is to get better ranked in the search engine for more targeted eyeballs.

▪Kickstarter

Kickstart is a crowdfunding platform where authors can create an online campaign to financially support their projects.

▪Kill Fee

Definition: Money paid to a writer in compensation for time spent working on assignment on a piece the publisher decides not to accept.

◊Kindle

According to the Huffington Post, the bestselling product ever on Amazon.com as of the time of publication is the Kindle, a hand-held electronic book reader with a monochrome screen. The Kindle's selling points include the fact that onscreen text is legible in bright sunlight and that the battery lasts for up to 30 hours of reading. The Kindle has access to a library of nearly 1 million books, and the 3G version of the device can download any title in approximately one minute from any location where it can receive a cell signal. Amazon.com has not released exact sales figures for the Kindle. Read more at:

http://www.ehow.com/info_8672033_amazoncom.html#ixzz2zAuPanLM

◊Kindle Cloud Reader

Kindle books can be read without a Kindle. This service enables people to read ebooks by using Firefox, Chrome, and Safary browsers on macintosh, iOS, Windowa, Linuz, and Chromebook devices.

◊Kindle Countdown Deals

Kindle book's sales are potentially maximized by choosing between two favorable promotional tools. Kindle Countdown Deals is a time-bound discount marketing strategy for a book, available on Amazon.com and Amazon.co.uk, while earning royalties. There's also the *Free Book Promotion* where readers worldwide can get a free book for a limited time. Plus, the author can earn 70% royalty for sales to customers in Japan, India, Brazil, and Mexico. To qualify, the book must be enrolled in KDP Select. Visit KDP Select or the Kindle Owners' Lending Library.

◊Kindle Daily Nation

A website providing free Kindle books as well as Kindle tips, news, and commentary.

◊Kindle Direct Publishing

An Amazon self-publishing service and one of the major ebook resellers.

◊Kindle Fire HD

Description: The flagship line of Amazon's tablet products characterized by a color touch screen and powered by Android OS. The first generation Kindle Fire HD of Amazon's Kindle Fire line of touchscreen tablet computers was announced in September, 2012; available in two models, 7" and 8.9". On September 25, 2013, the 7" model was discontinued and the Fire HD second generation was released. The Fire HD 7" processor speed was changed to 1.5 GHz, upgraded from "Android based" to a proprietary fork named Fire OS 3. In addition the Fire successor, the Kindle Fire HDX, was introduced.

◊Kindle Paperwhite

Description: Amazon's line of backlit ebook readers. Compared to the original Kindle, the Paperwhite has 62% more pixels for unsurpassed resolution, 25% better contrast touchscreen with built-in light and long battery life. The innovative built-in light evenly illuminates the screen to provide the perfect reading experience in all lighting conditions, even sunlight.

◊Kindle Reading Apps

Free, installable apps offered by Amazon that can be used to read Kindle ebooks with tablets, phones, and computers.

◊Kindle Serials

An Amazon service that publishes books in a subscription type format. Readers pay one time and receive future installments automatically.

◊Kindle Singles

This term has currently evolved to simply mean short ebooks. They can be short stories, novellas, or nonfiction works offered by

Amazon for 99 cents to about $2.99.

◊Kindlegraph

Kindle ebooks can be autographed by the author using this service.. A special insertion and personalized message with digitized signature is possible.

○Kirkus Reviews

This service helps readers and resellers discover new books. It also provides editing services.

▪Kivar

Definition: A proprietary product used for hardcover books.

○Kobo

One of the major sellers of ebooks and ebook readers.

◊KOLL - Kindle Owners' Lending Library

With an Amazon Prime membership, Kindle owners can now choose from thousands of books to borrow for free once a month, with no due dates. With Amazon Prime, Kindle owners can choose from more than 500,000 books to borrow for free with no due dates, including over 100 current and former New York Times best sellers and all 7 Harry Potter books. An author can earn a share of the fund based on how frequently the book is borrowed. Currently, the Kindle Owners Lending library is available for readers in the following marketplaces: Amazon.com, Amazon.co.uk, Amazon.de, Amazon.fr, and Amazon.co.jp. In addition, by choosing KDP Select, you will have access to a new set of promotional tools, including Kindle Countdown Deals (limited time promotional discounting for your book) and Free Book Promotion (readers worldwide can get your book free for a limited time). Authors and publishers can enroll a single title, their whole catalog or anything in between within KDP Select. By enrolling your book in KDP Select, you will also be eligible to earn 70% royalty for sales to customers in Brazil, Japan, India, and Mexico.

L

▪Laminate

Definition: To bond a plastic film by heat and pressure to a printed sheet for protection and appearance.

▪Laser Printer

Description: A nonimpact output device that burns an image on paper through the use of a small laser.

▪LaTeX

A word processor or document preparation system that emphasizes content over appearance. The output is high quality for technical and scientific publications.

▪Lay Flat Binding

Description: A special process allowing a softcover book to fully open and lay flat so it does not snap shut.

▪Layout

Definition: The working template of proposed design for a printing job.

▪LCCN

The Library of Congress Control Number or LCCN is a serially based system of numbering cataloging records in the Library of Congress in the United States. It has nothing to do with the contents of any book, and should not be confused with Library of Congress Classification.

▪Leading

Definition: The amount of vertical spacing, measured in points, between lines of typeset text.

▪Leaflet

Definition: Printed paper sheet folded in the center to produce four pages.

▪Letter Press

Description: Printing from raised type rather than from photographic plates.

▪Library Edition

Description: A book with a reinforced binding.

◊Library Processing

Library Processing is an Amazon Service for Public and Academic Libraries across the United States. Librarians all over the world use this unique identifier in the process of cataloging most books which have been published in the United States. It helps them reach the correct cataloging data (known as a cataloging record), which the Library of Congress and third parties make available on the Web and through other media.

○ LibreOffice

The software is available for free, an open-source productivity suite that includes a word processor, spreadsheet, and other applications.

■ Licensing

A popular trend for self-published authors is selling either mass-market or trade paperback rights to a book. This will most likely be the largest sale in terms of financial gain. The phenomenon is intriguing but writers who initially discover trade publishers' doors closed to them are opting to self-publish strictly as a stepping stone. They realize that self-publishing can bring them forcefully to the attention of the conventional publishing community with high profitable, fame-producing results. The self-publisher's formula is to write the book, publish the book, make the book a success, then sell the book. It is being done time after time.

■ Light Table

Description: A table with a diffused light underneath to facilitate paste-up of text and artwork.

○ Lightning Source

The print-on-demand company owned by Ingram that offers authors low printing costs.

▪Liking

A term used on social media websites describing a method of approval for a post or brand (like on Facebook).

▪Limerick

A limerick is a form of poetry, especially one in five-line metrical foot (two short syllables followed by a long one) with a strict rhyme scheme, which is sometimes obscene with humorous intent. The first two lines rhyme with the last line and the third and fourth line rhyme, and they are usually shorter. The form can be found in England as of the early years of the 18th century. It was popularized by Edward Lear in the 19th century, although he did not use the term.

▪Limited Edition

Description: A specified and limited quantity of books, often numbered and signed by the author.

▪Line Art

A line drawing that is black and white or illustration with no gray tones not requiring screening.

▪Line Shot

Any negative, print, copy or printing plate that is composed of solid image areas without halftone patterns.

○ LinkedIn

Description: A social network oriented toward job hunting and business development.

▪ Links

Definition: An external connector for users to find other related brandings (and pins).

▪ Line Block

Description: Referencing Printing, Lithography & Bookbinding, a line block is a letterpress printing block made by a photoengraving process without the use of a screen.

▪ List

Definition: All of the titles a publisher has in print and for sale. Or the official, or listed retail price of a book (list price).

▪ List Broker

Description: Someone who handles direct-mail listing rentals for use in direct marketing campaigns.

◊ Listmania

Amazon Trademark, fabulous and effective marketing tactic, where the function is to basically create a *List* to let people know about books that have been found to be interesting. Rules change, but it may not be necessary to purchase books or items from *Amazon.com* to add to a list, but must have used your account to complete a purchase of an item. The requirement is to wait at least 24 hours after your first purchase before creating a List. The idea is to pick an interesting theme and add up to twenty-five products. When promoting a book, the tasks require products that appeal to a specific demographic and simultaneously attract as many consumers as possible. The list is created from an Author Profile Page, under the orange Contributions label and Lists folder tab.

▪ListServ

An electronic mailing list that sends messages to all the addresses on the list.

○LIT

A Microsoft reader file

○Literary-Guild

The Literary Guild of America is a mail order book club selling low cost editions of current books to its members. The Literary Guild was established in 1927 by Samuel W. Craig and Harold K. Guinzberg as a competitor to the Book of the Month Club established in the previous year. Craig asserted that he originally incorporated the company in 1922 and reincorporated it in 1926 after hearing of the success of book clubs in Germany. In 1929 they created a subsidiary operation, the Junior Library Guild, which continues to this day. Books are selected by an editorial board. The chairman was Carl Van Doren. The chosen books are printed in special editions identified by the Literary Guild imprint on the title page. They are published on the same date as the trade editions. Charter subscribers were to receive twelve books a year at half the price of the trade editions for an annual fee of eighteen dollars.

○ Literary-Market-Place

The LMP or LiteraryMarketPlace.com brings the power of automated searching to the world's largest, most complete database of the book publishing industry.

○ LMP

LMP stands for Literary Market Place, the directory of the book publishing industry.

◊ Local Community Citizen

Amazon.com emphasizes that they are a citizen of local communities as well as the planet. They are proud to be a part of many different communities around the world and constantly looking for ways to further reduce their environmental impact. They are contributing to the communities where their employees and customers live and innovating on behalf of customers with initiatives like frustration-free packaging. They are also building tools for nonprofits and NGOs while also dedicating homepage placements. They too donate use of dedicated payments technology to enable customers to offer support to communities in need, in times of disaster. For more information about their community and environmental activities, visit "Innovations for Our Planet" and "Amazon in the Community" pages.

▪Logo

Definition: A symbol or illustration used as an identifying mark by a business (similar to a trademark).

◊Look Inside the Book

Look Inside The Book is a feature that Amazon started in 2001. Look Inside is a free program which allows readers to search and preview Kindle or book samples by clicking on titles identified by a Look Inside arrow attached to the book cover image. When publishing on KDP, a Kindle title is automatically enrolled in the program within a week of the on-sale date. Look inside is a great way to merchandise or promote titles.

○LuLu

Launched in 2002, Lulu pioneered the self-publishing industry and paved the way for people around the world to publish books and bring them to market, while allowing authors to retain full control. Operating a global network, Lulu provides worldwide distribution so that authors can reach readers just about anywhere via print, e-readers and tablet devices. Lulu has enabled people in more than 225 countries and territories to self-publish nearly two million publications, including 1.5 million books. Lulu is also the innovative engine that powers Picture.com, which lets individuals and businesses celebrate life experiences and enrich relationships by creating custom, premium quality photo specialty products.

Authors are offered three different quality packages; Value, Standard, and Premium. Options apply in each category for binding (coil-bound, perfect-bound, or saddle-stitch), interior print (full color, black and white on white, and black and white on cream), and various book sizes to choose.

■Lurker

Description: A person who anonymously observes what everyone else is saying in a Web discussion group.

8 M-N-O

M

○MacBook Air

MacBook Air is a Macintosh laptop, notable for being very light, thin, and much less cumbersome than others.

○MailChimp

Description: Marketing service that handles subscriptions, campaigns, and analytics for e-mail newsletters.

▪Mail Fulfillment House

Description: A company that handles envelope stuffing, addressing, and mailing for a direct-mail campaign.

▪Mail Order

Description: A method of merchandising books directly to the consumer using ads in magazines and newspapers.

■Make Ready

Description: An industry command phrase to make the printing press setup prepared and ready for a print run.

■Manuscript

Definition: A text of a book in a word-processor format. Normally prepared in double space for editing markups, the manuscript is refined, polished, and reworked several times until ready for the publishing stage.

■Margin

Definition: The edge surrounding the printed image on a page.

■Marketing Plan

Description: A publisher's total promotional plan for a book, including reviews, subsidiary rights, advertising and other customer contact.

■Marketing Research

Description: Information gathering and analysis relating to any aspect of marketing.

○Marketing Services

Marketing is the process of communicating the value of a product or service to customers, for the purpose of selling that product or service. Marketing Services are commercially available for publishers. Examples follow...

Rufus Space Industries Inc. in Columbia, SC 29201

The first step is to submit a Press Release to *Get Your News in Front of Major News Sites.* Companies like this one usually offer: Internet Advertising Service, Advertising Services, Advertising Marketing Services, Extreme Advertising Services, and Ad Agency Services.

www.TopWebsitePlacement.com

Marketers claim the best publicity is to secure Top Placement on Major Search Engines. This company predicts unlimited traffic with a Flat Price and a Month to Month Agreement. The first step is to Email contact information for more details.

CandiAdams@topwebsiteplacement.com

AceCo Publishers

(Email: acecoinc@west.net) www.cleandrivingrecord.com (Radio Publicity Digital E-Book)

▪Market Strategies

A very popular industry theory states that 80 percent of a publisher's results come from 20 percent of their efforts. Sadly, it is true that 80 percent of book sales are completely out of your hands. If Amazon.com, as an example, shows interest in your book, they'll work hard to promote it in places like search engine results, the "Customers Also Bought" section, top category lists, and targeted e-mail campaigns. The following promotional techniques show an industry conversion rate for book marketing strategies.

1. **Free Offer** to loyal fans and twitter followers   0.00% CR

2. **SlideShare** presentations (builds e-mail list)   0.00% CR

3. **CTA** (call to action at the book's end)   6.52% CR

4. **Email** to Author Page (via *autoresponder*)   12.5% CR

5. **Sidebar Sticky Widget** (clicks vs. sales)   11.3% CR

6. **Menu Link** (clicks vs. sales)   8.2% CR

7. **Blind E-mail Link** (special deals)   8.6% CR

8. Website "**Thank-You**" page   15.0% CR

9. **Hello Bar** (Blog plugin)   16.2% CR

10. **Facebook** (Organic specific groups)   17.7% CR

11. **E-mail** (Large List)   17.9% CR

12. **Group Author Event**   89.2% CR

13. **In Content** Blog Links   16.8% CR

14. E-mail **Last Chance** offer   18.0% CR

15. **99 cent** Book launch via E-mail   21.2% CR

Mass Customization

Description: Using digital printing to place different names, text or images in each book.

Mass Market Paperback

Mass Market Paperback is the smaller 4 x7 paperback designed for the widest possible distribution.

Master

Definition: The original camera-ready artwork.

◊MatchBook

Any KDP title that has a print version and that is sold by Amazon.com is eligible for the Kindle MatchBook program The Kindle MatchBook program offers customers who purchase, or have previously purchased, a print book from Amazon.com the option to purchase the Kindle version of that title for $2.99 or less. If you have a print version of your title and enroll the Kindle version in Kindle MatchBook you can earn a royalty from Kindle Direct Publishing (KDP) based on the Promotional List Price (choose from $2.99, $1.99, $0.99, or free) for any Kindle MatchBook sale.

▪Match-Print

Description: A proof for four-color process work to show color done properly.

▪Matte Finish

Matte Finish is a non-glossy finish. A glossy finish is a better choice for those who want to print and maintain everyday color photos while matte finish is better if you want to feature black & white or sepia. Glossy is shiny with bright colors and the images are sharp and show fine detail while matte finish is a highly textured print and it doesn't glare and doesn't reflect light.

▪Mechanical Binding

Description: The binding assembly using wire, staples, or plastic.

▪Media

Print, broadcast, recording and other methods for delivering messages to the market.

▪Media Angles

Media angles are the basic talking points that a publicist uses to convince the media to arrange for an author's interview or cover the book. The media angle is similar to sales handles that together, help clinch a deal with a producer or reporter to get a new title covered.

▪Media Escorts

For key authors, a media escort (nicknamed author-hailer) is hired in each market or city, by the publicist to assist and escort authors to scheduled events. That person meets the author at the airport, takes them to all of their media appearances, book signings, radio shows; whatever is on the publicity schedule. They are there to handle any problems that may arise, including confusion about bookings (there are all kinds of things that can go wrong). Naturally the escorts know the local media very well. They often do extra things such as help them to deal with small personal issues. They are a driver, pal, assistant, and publicist during the days spent with the author.

▪Media Flyer

Description: A brochure designed to be sent to talk shows.

▪Metadata

Metadata is ancillary information embedded in an ebook file. It includes the cover, title, author, copyright, and ISBN of an ebook.

▪Microblog

Description: A form of weblog allowing subscribers to broadcast brief messages to others on the service, often via a mobile device, and generally limited to 140 characters. Twitter is the best-known microblog.

▪Microfiche

Description: One of three major microforms (microfilm, microfiche, microfarads) in which information is stored in reduced form on photographic film and read through a special enlarging device.

▪Microfiche Cards

Description: A flat-surface film in card size. Many wholesalers periodically send their inventory listings on microfiche to bookstores.

○Microsoft Word

Description: Microsoft's word-processing software is the most prevalent in use today.

▪Midlist

Midlist is a professional author who has steady, but not strong sales.

▪Midlist Book

Any titles not at the top of the publisher's priorities is referred to as a midlist book. When this is the case, an author stands little chance of persuading a publisher to spend the kind of money required for print ads and other paid media.

○Midwest Book Review

An organization that reviews books while giving priority consideration to small publishers, self-published authors, academic presses, and specialty publishers.

▪MOBI

A standard ebook file format used by Amazon and Kindle.

○MobileRead

Description: An online discussion board focussing on the reading of books using mobile devices. Topics include ebook readers, ebook apps, and ebook formats.

▪Mockup

In book publishing and design, a mockup, or mock-up, is a full-size model, used for teaching, demonstration, promotion, and other purposes. A prototype provides at least part of the functionality and enables evaluation of a design. Mock-ups are used by designers mainly to acquire feedback from users. Mock-ups address the idea captured in a popular engineering one-liner: "You can fix it now on the drafting board with an eraser or you can fix it later on the construction site with a sledge hammer."

▪Model Release

Model release is a written authorization or a form giving permission to use a photograph of an individual for publication.

▪Monograph

A monograph is a short written report covering a single specific subject. Book publishers use the term "artist monograph" to indicate books consisting of reproductions of works of art by a single artist, as opposed to surveys of art from multiple artists.

▪Moodboard

A Mood Board (sometimes referred to as an Inspiration Board) is used in several different disciplines. Designing a book cover requires a compilation of inspirational elements as well. Another example is a mood board that can be extremely useful by establishing the aesthetic feel for a web site. It basically fits into the process somewhere after wireframes and before design mockups. Things that can be explored include photos, color palettes, typography, patterns, and the overall look and feel of the site. A rough color collage with textures is all that it takes to evoke a specific style or feeling. The mood board is intentionally casual to let the designer begin with broad ideas and get feedback before too much effort is invested. Many think of it as a rapid visual prototype.

◊Montlake Romance

Description: An Amazon imprint that publishes contemporary, suspense, paranormal, and historical romance titles.

▪Multimedia Content

Multimedia are features such as those found in Multi-Touch books, including graphics, photos, links, movies, animations, and user-interaction elements such as self-assessment quizzes.

▪Multiple Submissions

Description: The offering of a work to more than one publisher at the same time.

▪Multipurpose

Definition: An industry expression that means spinning off additional editions of the manuscript, hardcover, softcover, audio, eBook, etc.

▪Multi-Touch ebook

Description: Books available for iPads that contain multimedia content.

▪MS

MS is an abbreviation for "manuscript".

○ **MySpace**

A free access social networking Internet site that was once the most popular community.

N

◊NaNoWriMo

Description: The month of November is National Novel Writing Month. (NaNoWriMo): http://nanowrimo.org

○Nan A. Talese

Nan A. Talese is a literary imprint committed to quality publishing, both in the excellence of its authors and the quality of the production of its books. Established in 1990, it is distinguished both by new authors of fiction and nonfiction, as well as the authors Mrs. Talese has published for many years, writers who have been staunchly supported by independent booksellers (and more recently Barnes & Noble and Borders) and reviewers. Among its writers are Peter Ackroyd, Margaret Atwood, Pinckney Benedict, Thomas Cahill, Kevin Canty, Lorene Cary, Pat Conroy, Jennifer Egan, Mia Farrow, Antonia Fraser, David Grand, Nicola Griffith, Aleksandar Hemon, Thomas Keneally, Alex Kotlowitz, Robert MacNeil, Ian McEwan, Gita Mehta, George Plimpton, Edvard Radzinsky, Mark Richard, Nicholas Shakespeare, Barry Unsworth, and Gus Van Sant.

○NBCC

NBCC stands for the National Book Critics Circle which was founded in April 1974 at the Algonquin Hotel in New York City. Founding members included John Leonard, Nona Balakian, and

Ivan Sandrof. Their intentions were to extend the Algonquin round table to a national conversation. The NBCC gained 501(c)(3) status in October 2006, and in 2010 received an NEA grant to support the website and its literary blog. The NBCC serves nearly 600 member critics, authors, literary bloggers, book publishing personnel, and student members. Membership in the NBCC is open to freelance and staff book reviewers at various stages in their careers, associate nonvoting members, and student members. Full members receive access to tips on book reviewing, an annually updated guide to publications that accept freelance pitches for reviews and the ability to nominate titles for their annual awards. In addition, full membership grants electing board members, access to members-only discussion groups, plus a variety of discounts on literary magazines.

NetGalley

Netgalley.com is an author and publisher service for marketing and delivering ebooks to professional reviewers, bloggers, and journalists.

New American Library

The New American Library (**NAL**) is an American publisher based in New York. Since 1948, its focus is affordable paperback reprints of classics and scholarly works, popular and pulp fiction. Non-fiction, original and hardcopy issues are also produced.

New Press

The New Press is a nonprofit public-interest book publisher. Financial gifts (tax-deductible donations) support **The New Press** in continuing to leverage books for social change. Published books promote and enrich public discussion and understanding of the issues vital to democracy and to a more equitable world.

Nexus7

Nexus is a tablet offered by Google.

Niche

A niche market is a specific topic focusing which defines features aimed at satisfying needs of the demographics that it is intended to impact.

Noir

Description: The term originates from stories in the Prohibition-period in America describing the atmosphere written by hardboiled writers in the early 1940s. Some were adapted for screen-plays in *Film noir*, a French cinematic term, by the Austro-German film-making emigrants in Hollywood who fled the similarly corrupt system in Europe which allowed for the Nazi movement to gain power.

Nonphoto Blue

Description: A light blue pencil or ink that will not be picked up by a plate-making camera. Light blue pens and pencils are used to mark pasted up sheets and also called nonrepro blue.

Nook Media LLC

Nook e-reader is a Barnes & Noble product. In 2012, Microsoft entered into an agreement to create this new company, investing over $600 million for an 18 percent share. The new company owns the Nook e-reader, the Barnes & Noble College Bookstore, and the Barnes & Noble college marketing service.

▪Nothing Binding

Nothing Binding is a network of authors, readers, publishers, and book enthusiasts. The social media's purpose and goal is breaking "the chains of the current publishing dinosaur system that's blocking the great wave of literary progress, learning and enjoyment."

▪Notch Binding

Description: A binding process where the spines are not cut from the signatures but instead notches are cut down each spine and, with signatures still intact, the cover glued on.

▪Novel

A novel is a fictional style narrative in the form of a story of considerable length, typically having a plot that is unfolded by the actions, speech, and thoughts of the characters.

○NPH

NPH stands for Nazarene Publishing House, the publishing arm of the Church of the Nazarene, is the largest publisher of Wesleyan-Holiness literature in the world. and has been located in Kansas City, Missouri since its foundation in 1912. NPH prints more than 25 million pieces of literature each year, and processes more than 250,000 orders annually from more than 11,000 churches.

○**NPR**

NPR stands for National Public Radio; a multimedia news organization that focuses on unbiased and in-depth journalism.

■**Nth Name**

Description: Incrementally selected names from a mailing list, such as every 10th name used in testing lists.

O

▪OCR

OCR stands for Optical Character Recognition; a device or computer software that can recognize (read) typewritten characters and convert them to electronic impulses for translation to output media language. An OCR reader can read a printed page into a computer for editing.

▪OEB

OEB stands for Open E Book, a file format for eBooks.

▪Offset Printing

Offset printing is the traditional ink-press printing and a universally used technique. The inked image is transferred (or *offset*) from a plate to a rubber blanket, then onto the printing surface. A traditional method used includes a combination of the lithographic process based on the repulsion of oil and water. The offsetting also utilizes a flat image carrier where the image to be printed obtains ink from ink rollers, while the non-printing area attracts a water-based film called a fountain solution. This keeps the non-printing areas ink-free. The modern *web* process feeds a large reel of paper through a huge press machine in several parts, which then prints continuously as the paper is fed through.

○On-Line-ebook reseller

The ebook digital reseller service works on behalf of an author. The current major online ebook resellers are: Kindle Direct Publishing (KDP Amazon), the iBookstore (Apple), PubIt (Barnes & Noble), Google Play (Google), and Kobo.

○On-Line-Labels

A website offering a variety templates is http://www.onlinelabels.com.

Publishers recommend that authors place labels on their own books stating they are a "local-author". The notice on the cover sparks interest from prospective neighborhood book lovers.

▪OOP

OOP means out of print book which is no longer available through the publisher.

▪OOS

OOS refers to out of stock and means not available because of supply that's temporarily exhausted.

◊Omnivoracious

Amazon Trademark: Omnivoracious is a blog run by the Books editors at Amazon.com. The website is under construction but aims to share passion for the written word through news and reviews.

▪**O**paque

Definition: Not admitting light or allowing light to pass through. For reproductions, it is the process of painting out parts of negatives so they will not be copied.

○**O**penOffice Writter

Description: An open-source word processor that comes included in the **OpenOffice** productivity suite and analogous to Microsoft Word or WordPerfect.

◇**O**penSearch

Amazon Trademark: OpenSearch is a collection of simple formats for the sharing of search results. **OpenSearch** formats help people discover and use search engines and to syndicate search results across the web. Created by A9.com, an Amazon.com company, the OpenSearch format is now in use by hundreds of search engines and search applications around the Internet. The specification is made available according to the terms of a *Creative Commons* license so that everyone can participate; see

http://www.opensearch.org

○**O**pen Source

The software product is available free and can be used in any way. Description: Open source refers to a general public coded computer program which can be used and modified from its original design. The program is typically created as a collaborative effort in which computer operators improve upon and even share changes within a community.

Operating System

Definition: A group of controlling programs that govern the functioning of a whole computer system. The operating system is an essential component of the system software in a computer system. Application programs essentially require an operating system to function.

Opinion Molders

Description: People who lead thought, such as authors, editors, celebrities and other high-profile people.

Optimal Images

Description: The ideal image size for document pages, determined according to the screen size of the reading device used. Images are not necessarily a problem if there's no need to modify before uploading and/or it has a very high resolution. One thing to keep in mind is that a lot of image editing software defaults to medium quality; meaning that JPGs could be on the blurry side from the get-go.

Then there are PNGs; images that typically have much larger file sizes and are very high quality. Unfortunately, this means they load a lot slower for users. Fortunately, lossless data compression means one can duplicate and save the image without losing any quality. When comparing a JPG and PNG side by side, the JPG tends to blur when there is text or signage involved. PNGs maintain a sharpness and clarity that a JPG just can't match. They also allow for transparent backgrounds, making them ideal for icons and logos. Here are a couple of simple rules of thumb to abide by:

1. Use JPGs for high quality photos and when you don't need to make a lot of modifications to an image before uploading it (limit saves).

2. Use PNGs for photos with text, illustrations, signs, logos, and icons, and any image you want to have transparency.

▪OPM

OPM stands for Other People's Money. The industry slang has turned into a business term basically describing borrowing capital from elsewhere rather than risking using one's own.

▪Option

Definition: The right to purchase or sell, such as movie rights, for a specified price subject to a certain specified length of time. Also, the right a publisher may have, by previous contract, to bid on an author's subsequent books.

▪Ornament

Description: A decorative device in book design, such as a larger initial letter, rule line, or border. A headpiece (also spelled head-piece), is an ornament or decoration printed in the blank space at the beginning of a chapter or other division of a book, usually an ornamental panel. These particular elaborate printer's ornament are done by a professional illustrator.

▪Orphan

Description: A hallmark of poor page layout. In typesetting, orphans differ from widows in that they are words or short lines at the beginning of a paragraph, which are left dangling at the top of a column, separated from the rest. There's disagreement about the definitions of widow and orphan; what one source calls a widow another calls an orphan. Either way, here are the noticeable displays of poor page layout.

(1) The first line of text in a paragraph is separated from the rest of the paragraph by a page break or new column.

(2) A word or part of a word that is not long enough to clear the indent of the following paragraph is by itself on the last line of a paragraph.

▪Otabind

Description: A trademark binding process for trade paperbacks that resembles perfect binding, having a printable spine, but allowing a book to be opened flat; ideal for cookbooks. In the past few years this process has come into use especially on the European continent. Otabind is named after the man who devised the process. Eurobinding, as the British prefer to call it, is credited to a 1981 patent by Mr. Ota, owner of the Finnish firm of Otavia. The license for the process was sold to the Dutch firm of Hexspoor, who are now its main practitioner and proponent.

The principle of Otabind is that the book-block is not glued to the spine, but instead to a sheet of substrate. The block is then fixed to the cover sheet by glueing it to the first and last pages of the book-block. These first and last leaves then loose much possibility of use – a significant portion of the inside-edge area is eaten up – and on the front and back cover the inside edges are scored to assist opening. A cover design will have to take account of that. When glueing is good (the cold-glue process can be used here too) and the sections are thread-sewn, Otabind can give nice results. In North America, a variation of the Otabind process goes under the name of RepKover. Among users of the technique, the publisher of computing books, O'Reilly, has much praise for it. Clearly, for text books that have to stay open on a desk, while the reader/user is busy at a keyboard, such a technique is useful.

▪Out of Print

Description: An industry phrase claiming a book is not available.

▪Out of Stock

Description: An industry phrase claiming a book is temporarily not available because the publisher's supply has been interrupted.

▪Output Format

An output format is a file produced during conversion. When a word DOC is converted to an EPUB file, the output format is EPUB, for example.

○Outskirts Press

A vanity publishing company that offers writing services, publishing packages, and marketing. The author maintains full control and 100 percent royalties but pays upfront for services rendered.

▪OverDrive

OverDrive is a description of a digital-content distributor of ebooks and audiobooks that focuses on the school and library market.

▪Overrun

An Overrun is an extra amount of finished copies of a book that the printer may produce above the stipulated order (should never exceed ten percent). Also, an additional quantity of book covers a publisher may order for promotional purposes.

▪Over the Transom

Over the transom refers to unsolicited material sent to a publisher directly by the author rather than through an agent or at the request of an editor.

○Oxbridge Communications, Inc.

The New York communications company (Oxbridge Communications, Inc.) maintains the largest database of U.S. and Canadian periodicals and catalogs-magazines, newsletters, newspapers, journals, directories, and catalogs. They offer subscribers options.

1. MediaFinder: This is their digital and online version of the extensive database.
   a. MediaFinder Full Service: Customers can search targeted groups.

b. MediaFinder Keyword Service: A stand-alone service to locate publishers by title, subject, or keywords.

c. MediaFinder CD: The available format comes out and available on an annual basis.

2. Four print directories are produced annually.

a. *Standard Periodical Directory*: The bible of the research community

b. *Oxbridge Directory of Newsletters*: The largest newsletter directory

c. *National Directory of Magazines*: Since 1988

d. *National Directory of Catalogs*: Since 1990

9 P-Q

P

▪Packing Slip

Description: A document sent with a shipment of books itemizing the contents of the shipment.

○Pages

Pages is an Apple word processor and page-layout application.

▪Pagination

Pagination is the numbering or order of pages in a book.

○Palibro

Palibro is an author-services imprint of Author Solutions.

○Pantheon

Pantheon's founder, Kurt Wolff, was born in Germany in 1887 to a Catholic father and a Jewish mother. He studied German literature and in 1913, founded Kurt WolffVerlag. The deteriorating German economic conditions forced Wolff to close

Kurt Wolff Verlag in 1930, and the changing political climate resulted in his decision to emigrate in 1933. He spent several years in France and then in Italy, where he became publishers of Pantheon Case Editrice, which he had co-founded in 1924. Wolff and his wife, Helen, emigrated to the United States in 1941. Within a year, they founded Pantheon Books in a one-room office in lower Manhattan. Wolff specialized in publishing literature in translation. He also published important works on art history. In 1961, Bennett Cerf bought Pantheon and it became a part of Random House. Today, Pantheon is part of the Knopf Doubleday Publishing Group and continues to publish world-class literature. Pantheon's authors include Julia Glass, James Gleick, Ha Jin, Anne Morrow Lindbergh, Alexander McCall Smith, Marjane Satrapi, Art Spiegelman, and Studs Terkel.

■Paragraph Styles

Paragraph styles is a feature used in word processing to tag paragraphs with specific style options such as font, size, color, and alignment. Changes to the paragraph style automatically affect all paragraphs in the document tagged with that style.

○Paramount Books

Paramount Publishing Enterprise was established in 1948. Today, it enjoys the status of being one of Pakistan's leading publishers and booksellers. They serve not only as exclusive distributors but also reprint books under license in Pakistan from some renowned international companies like Letterland, UK and Cambridge University Press, India.

▪Party

A book party customarily launches a new title. Some in the industry believe it gauche to sell books at a party. Pragmatic people will take a sale anywhere. For the big-timers, a publisher would be involved and then the publicist brings books to give away or sell.

▪Paste-Up

Description: An array of reproduction-quality copy arranged in proper position on a paper (board) prepared as line copy ready for the camera, sometimes referred to as mechanical.

▪PDF

Also referred to as Portable Document Format, pdf is a static-page file designed to mimic a printed page.

▪Peer Review

Description: The manuscript editing by an expert in the subject field.

▪Pen Name

Description: Also referred to as "Pseudonym" is an assumed name to conceal an author's identity. The Amazon Author Central account allows you to click on "BOOKS", then "Add more books". Then search for another book that you have under a pen name, then click on "This is my book". It will then ask if you want to add a pen name, in which case, you'll have to contact Amazon and let them know. It's fairly easy to do and up to 3 pen names per account are allowed at the moment.

■Perfect Binding

Description: The standard glued-on cover seen on most softcover books. It has a squared-off spine on which the title and name of the author may be printed.

■Periodical

A Periodical is a magazine, newspaper, or other publication with a fixed interval between issues.

■Permission

Definition: An authorization from a copyright holder to quote material or reproduce illustrations taken from the copyrighted work which often requires a fee.

■Permission Marketing

Description: To combat undesirable interruption techniques, all marketing agents will obtain permission before advancing to the next step in the purchasing pitch. For example, they ask if it would be alright to send email newsletters to prospective customers. This method is mainly used by online marketers, notably email marketers and search marketers, as well as certain direct marketers who send a catalog in response to a request. Marketers feel this is a more efficient use of resources because the offers are sent to people only if actually interested. This is one technique used that has an effective personal orientation. Marketers feel that marketing should be done on a one-to-one basis rather than using broad aggregated concepts used in other industries.

○ Perseus Books

Perseus Books Group, an American publishing company founded in 1996 by investor Frank Pearl, was named Publisher of the Year in 2007 by Publishers Weekly magazine. The award was based on the company's significant role in taking on publishers formerly distributed by Publishers Group West and acquiring Avalon Publishing Group. Perseus Book Group also purchased Avalon Publishing Group, the parent company of Carroll & Graf and Thunder's Mouth Press.

■ PhotoComposition

Description: Setting type photographically by exposing a photo-sensitive paper or film to images of typed characters, in such a sequence as to create the desired text or copy.

■ Photodirect

Definition: Exposing an image directly to a light-sensitive offset plate material.

■ Photomechanical Transfer

PMT (photomechanical transfer) is a diffusion transfer process in which the paste-up is exposed to a sheet of sensitized paper. Then the paper is processed in contact with a receiver sheet, before the sheets are peeled apart to produce a usable image on the receiver.

▪Photostat

Photostat or stat is a photographic reproduction that can be negative or positive and made from film, artwork, other stats, etc., and used as line art for many art applications. The Photostat machine, or Photostat, was an early projection photocopier. The "Photostat" name, which was originally a trademark of the company, became generalized, and was often used to refer to similar machines and manufactured processes.

▪Phototypesetting

Description: A common form of typesetting where each character and word is a photographic image. Major advantages for this technique are crispness, economy, and speed.

▪PI

An abbreviation that means per inquiry advertising. The media provides the space or time for free but gets to take a piece of each sale.

▪Pica

A printing industry unit of measure equal to approximately 1/6 of an inch. There are 12 points to the pica usually used to measure width.

◊Pick Ambassadors

Pick ambassadors are employees that collect order items in warehousing. They walk ten miles a day retrieving items, serving 19.5 million customers daily (Florida population).

○ PID (publisher website ID)

PID is used to identify the publisher's website. A CJ publisher may have multiple PIDs under one single **CJ** account (e.g. if you maintain multiple websites, you will have multiple PIDs).

○ Pin / pinning

Description: Act of sharing content with video or image that gets posted (usually referring to Pinterest). Pinning too many topics on one board is annoying to users and will lower publisher's reputation.

○ Pinboard

Description: A Pinterest board having one very specific topic only which may attract less but targeted people is an advantage (quality over quantity). Google also indexes individual boards so it is wise to be sure descriptions are used wisely. Pinterest boards contain many theme based pins:

1. Pin it button: (add onto website for sharing)

2. Repin: (reposting someone else's pin)

3. Pinner: (person who pins)

○ Pinpuff.com

Description: A website for the publishing industry in conjunction with Pinterest. Influence characteristics measure success and failures of pins and boards. Quick Stats shows the number of Followers, Followings, Pins, Boards, Likes, Repins, and Liked.

○ PinReach.com

Description: A website that helps monitor trends and statistics and gives publishers an idea of how to grow a following (where you stand, how many followers you have, etc.); similar to Pinpuff but better graphics.

○ Pinterest

A Trademark software company book-marketing (social media) website: *Pinterest Board / Pin-it Button*. It operates on an invite-only system. This has created a viral desire for people to get invites from their friends (G-mail began this way, as an example). Some pay to get invited by using the "fiverr" website - Express Gigs tab with collections related to "pinterest invites". Five accounts on one invite are possible, but you can invite yourself using one account over and over, ideally for publishers and authors. The other possibility is to look for *Pinterest Invite Forums* on the internet.

■ Pitch

Discussion: Writers need to get across to the reader the promise of what reading their book will deliver. Generally, an important step in the book promotion is the all-important two- or three-sentence summary of the author's writing project. This has a dual purpose: to describe the book's genre and basic premise, and to intrigue the interested party. The whole idea is to sell the story instead of selling the book. A well-crafted **pitch** tantalizes with a hook that sets the manuscript apart from the rest.

There's a lot to pack into a couple of sentences, so choose words wisely. This may sound complicated and difficult, but it isn't. Read the movie descriptions in the local TV guide, or pick up a favorite novel and read the jacket or flyleaf copy. For example, identify this bestseller: "This is a family saga that begins with a birth in 1750 in an African village and ends seven generations later at the Arkansas funeral of a black professor whose children include a teacher, a Navy architect, and an author." Or this one: "Set in Depression-era Louisiana, this serialized novel is a prison guard's account of events that challenge his most cherished beliefs in the place of ultimate retribution: death row." These pitches came from the back covers of Alex Haley's Roots and Stephen King's The Green Mile.

Expert Advice: Do not pitch authors, pitch issues. Don't pitch books, pitch shows. Pitch letters should convey what the book offers an audience or readership.

◊Placeholders

Amazon adds a generic graphic referred to as a Placeholder which is added to books that are missing a product image. This happens on a weekly basis, so it will take up to one week to see the placeholder image. To replace the graphic, find the book you want to add an image to within the Amazon KDP bookshelf, and click the "Actions" button, then "Edit book details." You can upload an image in the Product Image section. After submission, it will go live after passing the review.

▪Plagerism

Definition: Copying another author's work and passing it off as one's own. To be proven, the actual words have to have been copied. In other words, one cannot plagiarize ideas or plots.

▪Plate

Description: A printing plate device bearing the image to be printed which can be paper, plastic, or metal.

▪Platform

Platform is marketing slang describing the sum total of people known who also know you, including, among others, friends and followers on social-media websites, e-mail contacts, readers of blogs or previous books, bloggers, reviewers, other authors, and people who have seen you speak.

▪Plog

Plog's are blog's with portable media sources like found in a *PodCast*. Characteristics are I-dependant audio, video and text weblog or a blog designed for full features, and the portability and ability to express and/or respond to ideas more effectively.

▪Plugging

Description: A print media condition where photos appear muddy or characters are filled-in caused by poor plate burning, over application of ink or an incorrect ink/water balance.

○Plugin

Plugin is a small software program that extends the functionality of a software application.

▪PMA

The abbreviation stands for Publishers Marketing Association which is a trade association that sponsors co-op promotions to help members sell books.

▪PMS color

Description: The Pantone Matching System for specifying specific shades of color. The proprietary color space is used in a variety of industries, primarily printing. The idea behind the **PMS** is to allow designers to "color match" specific colors. For example, the system is almost always used when a design enters production stage, regardless of the equipment used to produce the color. This coordination has been widely adopted by graphic designers and reproduction and printing houses. Pantone recommends that PMS Color Guides be purchased annually, as their inks become yellowish over time. Color variance also occurs within editions based on the paper stock used (coated, matte or uncoated), while interdictions of color variance occurs when there are changes to the specific paper stock used.

▪PO (Purchase Order)

A PO is a document used to purchase products and books.

○Pocket Books

Pocket Books is a division of Simon & Schuster that primarily publishes paperback books. They produced the first mass-market, pocket-sized paperback books in America in early 1939 and revolutionized the publishing industry.

▪POD

POD means print on demand which is a current technique of printing only as many books as are needed at the moment (fill an order). Print on demand with digital technology is used as a way of printing items for a fixed cost per copy, regardless of the size of the order. While the unit price of each physical copy printed is higher than with offset printing, the average cost is lower for very small print runs, because setup costs are much higher for offset printing.

While build to order has been an established business model in many industries, "print on demand" developed only after digital printing began, because it was not economical to print single copies using traditional printing technology such as letterpress and offset printing. Many traditional small presses have replaced their traditional printing equipment with POD equipment or contract their printing out to POD service providers. Many academic publishers, including university presses, use POD services to maintain a large backlist; some even use POD for all of their publications.[2] Larger publishers may use POD in special circumstances, such as reprinting older titles that are out of print or for performing test marketing.

Profits from print on demand publishing are on a per-sale basis. Royalties vary depending on the outsourcing route by which the item is sold. Larger profits usually come from sales direct from the print-on-demand service's website. A riskier method is when the author buys copies from the service at a discount, acting as the publisher, and then sells them personally. Lower royalties come from traditional "bricks and mortar" bookshops and online retailers both of which buy at high discount, although some POD companies allow the author to set their own discount level. Unless the author has fixed their discount rate, the higher the volume sold the lower the royalty becomes, as the retailer is able to buy at greater discount.

Because the per-unit cost is typically greater with POD than with a print run of thousands of copies, it is common for POD books to be more expensive than similar books that come from conventional print runs, especially if that book is produced exclusively with POD instead of using POD as a supplemental technology between print runs.

Book stores order books through a wholesaler or distributor, usually at high discount of anything up to 70 percent. Wholesalers obtain their books in two ways; either as a special order where the book is ordered direct from the publisher when a book store requests a copy, or as a stocked title which they keep in their own warehouse as part of their inventory. Stocked titles are usually also available via sale or return, meaning that the book store can return unsold stock for full credit at anything up to one year after the initial sale.

POD books are rarely if ever available on such terms because for the provider it is considered too much risk. However, wholesalers keep a careful eye on what titles are selling, and if authors work hard to promote work and achieve a reasonable number of orders from book stores or online retailers (who use the same wholesalers as the bricks and mortar stores), then there is a reasonable chance of their work becoming available on such terms. Although returns lessen the risk for book stores and helps POD authors get through the door, such authors should also realize there's only a certain stock that can be returned.

This difficulty with lack of returns can make bookstores less enthusiastic about POD books. This is set to change in the future. The book industry is currently debating a move away from sale or return altogether, which will tend to even things out. Another issue with print-on-demand titles is the fact that they are often debut works. Many book stores are reluctant to take a risk on an author's first, untested work without the endorsement of a commercial publisher.

▪Podcast

Description: A digital audio or digital programming that can he streamed over the Internet or downloaded to a computer or portable device.

▪Point

A vertical measurement used in typesetting. One point equals 1/72 of an inch.

▪POP display

Description: The book display racks, posters, bookmarks, and other sales materials given to bookstores or other retail outlets to promote a book (Dump).

▪Positive

Definition: A Photograph image in which the tones correspond to the original subject. A positive on paper is usually called a print.

▪Positioning

Positioning is a strategic placement of an ad or book where it will get maximum exposure. The word can also mean the place within a list where a book falls in relation to other titles or, in some cases, finding a special niche for a product.

▪Positioning Statement

Positioning statements are one or two appealing sentences that make listeners curious about a book. The idea behind the beginning proclamation is to create a way to talk about the book that will appeal to an audience, booksellers, the media, and readers. Generally, to come up with the opening statement, think about how to briefly answer the question, "What's your book about?" and "Who will read it?"

▪Posting

Description: A message entered into a network communications system, such as a newsgroup submission.

▪PostScript

Definition: A language for controlling printers and image setters.

▪PPI

PPI stands for pages per inch and used in measuring the paper thickness.

▪PPC

Pay per click (PPC) (industry known as *cost per click*) is an ad model. PPC directs traffic to websites where sellers pay the publisher (typically a website owner) when the advertisement is clicked. It is defined sometimes defined as "the amount spent to get an advertisement clicked."

▪PQN

PQN stands for **print quality needed** which refers to digital (toner) printing and not one at a time like POD.

▪Preface

The Preface is the introduction remarks usually by the author telling the reason the book was written and giving its aims and scope. In other words, it is part of a book's front matter.

▪Premium

Premium is a slang use that refers to a book that will be given away free as part of a promotional campaign for a product or service. Sometimes product or book links are advertised inside a book.

▪Prepack

Description: A point-of-purchase (POP) temporary counter or floor display often composed of cardboard and designed to hold and bring extra attention to merchandise.

▪Prepublication Price

Prepublication Price is basically a marketing technique using a special lesser price on a book bought before the official publication date. It is economically effective and used a lot.

▪Press Check

Description: When a customer is at the printing press in order to approve the job as it is printed which can last a few minutes or several days, depending on the job size.

▪Press Kit

A press kit, often referred to as a media kit in business environments, is a pre-packaged set of promotional materials of a person, company, or organization distributed to members of the media for promotional use. They are often distributed to announce a book release.

▪Press Release

A press release launches a title. Whether an author writes the press release or simply reviews the written release by a publicist, there are rules that need to be followed for success.

1. FOR IMMEDIATE RELEASE should appear at the top above a headline.

2. Contact name, phone number, and e-mail address to be stacked in the upper right-hand corner of the first page.

3. The headline is in capital letters and boldface, centered at page top to emulate a newspaper headline.

4. A dateline appears at the beginning of the first paragraph which also includes the news source location.

5. The first written paragraph presents the most important book information. Opportunity is lost if the most important and salient information is hidden deep inside the body.

6. Keep it to two pages maximum with double-spacing on letter-sized stationary.

7. Avoid sans-serif typefaces or others that are hard to read. The industry prefers Times New Roman or Garamond.

8. Mention any information of local interest in the lead paragraph.

9. Poor grammar and misspelled words disqualifies the release.

10. Include relevant quotes from the book that substantiates and reinforces the topic.

11. Avoid exclamation marks (looks amateurish!).

12. Do not use hyped-up words and phrases.

13. Keep sentences short.

14. Edit the press release ruthlessly to eliminate any redundancies or unnecessary text.

15. Compose the writing from a benefit viewpoint. In other words, clearly convey what the reader or consumer will gain from

reading the book.

16. After the first mention of the press release title, include in parenthesis the name of the publishing house and the publication date.

17. Book titles are conventionally written all in capital letters.

18. Names are written as Jim Smith the first time mentioned and as Smith of Mr. Smith afterwards.

19. At the center bottom, after the text body, type-30-or ### to indicate closure.

20. At the end of the release, list the publication date, page count, price, format (hardcover or paperback), publisher, and ISBN numbers. Also include the Web site address for the book, if any.

Additional information and professional help or assistance is available at http://www.directcontactpr.com/.

○Print-to-Order

The Lightning Source program that sells a book on an author's behalf and pays the author the difference between the wholesale price and printing costs.

○Print-to-Publisher

The Lightning Source program in which an author orders copies of his or her book from Lightning Source, which then ships copies of a manuscript to the author, wholesalers, retailers, and warehouses. These books appear to come from the author, who pays the company for the printing, handling, and shipping. The author then bills and collects from the recipients of the books.

▪Production Expenses

Description: Generally includes typesetting, key lining, printing, and binding.

▪Promotional Material

Description: Any printed matter such as fliers, catalog sheets, letters, review copies designed to publicize and sell books.

▪Proofs

Proofs created in a near-final version for editing and checking purposes are called page proofs. In the page-proof stage, mistakes are supposed to have been corrected; to correct a mistake at this stage is expensive, and authors are discouraged from making many changes to page proofs. Page layouts are examined closely in the page proof stage. Page proofs also have the final pagination, which facilitates compiling the index. In printing and publishing, proofs are the preliminary versions of publications meant for review by authors, editors, and proofreaders, often with extra-wide margins. Galley proofs may be uncut and unbound, or in some cases electronically published. They are created for proofreading and copyediting purposes, but may be used for promotional and review purposes also.

▪Proofreader

Proofreading is the reading of a galley proof or an electronic copy of a publication to detect and correct production errors of text or art. Proofreaders are expected to be consistently accurate by default, being the last stage of production before publication.

▪Proportion Wheel

Description: A small device used to determine enlargements and reductions for artwork.

▪Proportional Spacing

Description: A method of spacing in most typeset copy in which the width of a letter is determined by the actual amount of space it needs.

▪Proposal

Description: A detailed plan of a proposed new enterprise that is used to sell that project. Also, a package consisting of an outline, sample chapters, author bio, and other supporting materials used by a writer to persuade a publisher to offer a contract for a book.

▪Pseudonym

Definition: An assumed name used to conceal an author's identity. Also called a pen name.

▪Public Domain

Description: Text material that is not protected by copyright.

Publication Date

A Publication date is the determined day when a book's promotion is slated to peak and books are available for purchase. A launch date usually is set three to four months after the book is printed.

Publicist

A Publicist is an agent who prepares promotional materials and schedules media appearances either as an independent contractor or as part of the staff of a publisher, advertising agency, or PR firm.

Publisher

A publisher is the party who puts up the money, basically. If you invest in your own printing, you are a self-publisher. If you begin to take in manuscripts from others, you are a (small) publisher. If you grow, you become a large publisher. Your computer makes it easy and inexpensive to write, produce, publish and sell books. You can work from home and you do not need any governmental licenses. Self-publishing should not be confused with "Vanity" publishing.

Publishers Weekly

The news magazine is an industry periodical for publishers, librarians, booksellers, and literary agents. Probably the most popular trade news journal, **PW** is targeted at publishers, literary agents, booksellers, and librarians. The company has been around since 1872 with an emphasis on book reviews. In 2008, the magazine's circulation was 25,000. In 2004, the breakdown of those 25,000 readers was given as 6000 publishers; 5500 public libraries and public library systems; 3800 booksellers; 1600 authors and writers; 1500 college and university libraries; 950 print, film and broad media; and 750 literary and rights agents, among others.

Publishing House

The consumer book publishing business company that produces the publication of content that entertains, educates, and informs. Discrete functions are performed such as...

1. Content acquisition: acquiring an author's manuscript.

2. Development and manuscript enhancement.

3. Book design.

4. Production cycle management.

5. Prepress, printing and preparing the finished project.

6. Marketing campaigns.

7. Distribution channels.

8. Warehousing management.

9. Customer service.

10. Sub and foreign rights supervision.

Publishing Spring

The term was coined during the turning point in early 2012 when tablets and eReaders grew beyond an early-adopter fad. At that time the devices became a mainstream gift and Christmas present rage.

Publication Date

A Publication Date is a date, typically set three to four months after books are actually in-house and available. This date is the official launching.

▪Pubslush

Definition: A crowdfunding website dedicated to books.

▪Pure-Text Novel

Description: A novel that's composed entirely of text and no graphics.

◊Press Room

http://phx.corporate-ir.net/phoenix.zhtml?p=irol-mediaHome&c=176060

Amazon uses a selected web site to make announcements and present press releases concerning corporate deals, awards, earnings, Amazon demographics, technological advancements, and special writing competitions. For example, on April 30,2014, Amazon.ca and *Quilt & Quire Today* unveiled Wayne Grady as the winner for the 2013 First Novel Award.

○Pretty Link

A free Plugin (link cloaking plugins) available from http://wordpress.org. Makes links far more user friendly and professional looking. This download makes it easy to setup outbound links. It gives affiliates peace of mind knowing that their links can be tracked.

▪Publisher

A publisher refers to a company that publishes a book. The term *traditional publisher* explains an operation that has been going on for more than a century. This includes purchasing rights, royalties, advances, acquisition editors, designs, marketing, production, printing, shipping, sales, distribution, and decision-making. *Self-publishing* is a blanket term that encompasses many approaches, all of which are the author's responsibility (similar, in a way, like a building contractor who arranges work tasks).

Publishers

There are hundreds of book publishing establishments. The major companies with their specialties are listed as follows...

Scholarly Books

Cambridge University
Harvard University
Oxford University Press
Princeton University
Stanford University
University of Chicago
University of Toronto
Yale University Press

General Books

Wolters/Kluwer
Reed Elsevier
Spinger Science / Bus.

Trade

CBS (Simon & Schuster

Trade / Education

Houghton Mifflin Harcourt
John Wiley & Sons
Pearson PLC

Business / Professional

McGraw Hill
Thomas Renters (Lega

Purchasing Rights

A publisher purchases from the author the right to publish one or more books in various formats (hardcover, paperback, audio, etc.)

and in various territories (the whole world).

▪Print-ready PDF

A pdf that is intended to be submitted to an author-services company or print-on-demand company. The pdf file is used to produce printed books. Common characteristics of a print-ready pdf includes hyperlink text that is neither underlined nor colored differently from the surrounding text, and front matter consistent with *The Chicago Manual of Style*.

◊Prime

Amazon Prime is a *Shop with Point* FREE Two-Day Shipping available on millions of books and items. There's no minimum order size and there's unlimited instant streaming of thousands of movies and TV shows with Prime Instant Video. Consumers can also read free books each month through Kindle First and the Kindle Owners' Lending Library. Amazon.com may offer a 30-Day Free Trial. After your free trial, there's an annual fee but you can cancel anytime.

◊Privacy

Privacy is a legal Amazon Services **notice** which governs services and practices

◊Purchase Circles

Amazon Trademark and highly specialized best-seller lists covering what people are buying around the world, in your home-town, at various companies, for the government, even at your alma mater.

These lists are available by selecting "Purchase Circles" in the Special Features Menu. The lists can then be organized by geography, government, organizations (nonprofits, professionals), companies A-Z, or education A-Z. Example: conduct a regional marketing campaign with research of what is moving in New York versus Los Angeles versus Chicago – Houstan etc. Go to the Geography category, click on United States, then the city. Likewise, you can see what books certain companies are buying and if your new title fits.

▪PW Select

Description: A quarterly supplement to the regular edition of Publishers Weekly focused on self-publishing and containing listings and reviews of self-published books.

Q

○ Quantcast

Description: Audience oriented website (measures your audience for free). Check out a site profile to see the power of their reports (traffic, demographics, lifestyle, interests, etc.).

▪ Query Letter

Description: A one to two page letter created to interest an editor or agent in a book project or magazine article. Displays the author's writing ability and is meant to sell an idea. Also known as a query.

▪ Quick Printing

Description: Producing a printer plate or master directly from the original boards (paste-ups) to reproduce multiple copies.

○ Quill & Quire

Quill & Quire is a Canadian published magazine of book news and reviews.

▪Quote

Description: An endorsement for a book or price quote for printing. Or a statement, often from a celebrity or key reviewer, used in advertising or for book cover copy. Also, an exact copy of original wording from another source reproduced in one's own writing, enclosed in quotation marks. Also, an offer to do work for a specific sum of money, as in a price quote.

10 R-S

R

▪Ragged Right

Ragged Right is a right-hand margin that doesn't align evenly.

▪Ranking

Discussion: Authors who want to get serious about selling books and e-Books need to benchmark progress by monitoring and analyzing sales. Good marketers become better marketers when they can tell what happens to sales when they:

1. Change the price of their book.

2. Bought advertising

3. Changed the cover

4. Launched a publicity campaign

5. Initiated a blog tour

Categories to track depends more on what information is available, but it can include unit sales, samples downloads, borrows, free copies, print vs. e-Book format, etc.

▪Rate Card

Description: A price sheet giving the costs of media time or space advertising.

▪Reason to Buy a Book

Discussion: The publishing industry has determined seven relevant points in determining economic feasibility when consideration is given to a new book. Prospective book buyers, as a general rule, will make a decision based on these considerations. They are (in order of relevance) – author – genre – on major best seller lists – price – recommendations – book reviews – striking book cover.

▪Recto

Recto refers to a right-hand page, as opposed to a verso or left-hand page.

▪Recto-Veto

Description: Two-sided printing.

▪Reduction

Description: The photographic process of creating an image smaller than the original, or scaling an oversize copy for reduction. For example, a half-size image, which is a 50 percent reduction, or scale 50 percent, or three-fourths size image, which is scale 75 percent.

▪Register

Description: The correct positioning of print on a page or, in color process printing, proper positioning of separations relative to each other so everything appears crisp.

▪Remaindering

Remaindering is a publisher's selling of the remaining stock of unsuccessful books for a fraction of their list prices.

▪Reprint

Reprint is a general term used in publishing to describe any new printing of a book. It can also mean printing the book in another version, such as paperback in lieu of hardcover.

▪Repro

Description: A reproduction proof is camera-ready copy on photosensitive paper to be pasted up on mechanicals to be photographed.

▪Reseller

A company that acts as an intermediary between an author and his or her readers by stocking, marketing, and selling the author's work.

▪Retail Flipping

Retail flipping is a coined term describing a brand new business model where profits are produced when products are sold online.

There's a slight catch to this because acquiring inventory at retail prices and reselling online to make money requires a successful methodology. The opportunity exists to those who are willing to find retail products at the lowest price point, then simply know how to sell for a gain.

■Retail Price

Description: The price customers see and pay for the final version of a published book.

■Retouching

Description: Touch-up of a photograph to correct any flaws or to improve appearance.

■Returns

Returns are books or products that have not been sold and are sent back to a publisher for credit or a cash refund.

■Reverse

To print an image white on black, rather than black on white.

■Review

Definition: A critical evaluation of a work, citing strengths, weaknesses, or both.

■Review Copy

Description: A publisher's complimentary copy of a book forwarded to reviewers or potential wholesale purchasers.

▪Revised Edition

Revised Edition is a new edition of a previously published book containing updated or supplemental material.

▪Revisions

Changes and corrections made to a complete draft of a manuscript or set of proofs.

▪Rights

Rights are the various *rights* to reproduce or publish a work in any form, in whole or in part that its author may sell or retain. (First series rights, second serial rights).

▪Royalty

Discussion: All book-publishing royalties are paid by the publisher, who determines an author's funding rate, except when the author can demand high advances with royalties. The general concept is that the author receives a percentage of the revenue for each book sold. The exact percentage can't be generalized because it depends on a variety of factors: the size of the publisher, whether it's a CBA or ABA house, the author's platform and salability, and each publisher's own criteria. Hardback royalties on the published price of trade books usually range from 10% to 12.5%, with 15% for more important authors. On paperback it is in the neighborhood of 7.5% to 10%, going up to 12.5% only in exceptional cases.

Most publishers pay the royalty based on the cover price (or retail price) of the book. CBA publishers usually pay royalties based on the NET price of the book, that is, the price at which the publisher sold the book to the bookstore.

◊Royalty Payment Notification

A royalty payment notification is for Kindle Direct Publishing (KDP) sales recorded in the FR Kindle Store. Payment will be made to a specified bank account and should appear as am available balance within 2 to 5 business days after the Payment Date. Details of the payment will always be available on the Payment Report (https://kdp.amazon.com/self-publishing/reports) after it has been processed by the bank. Payment is based on 35% or 70% for Kindle ($2.99 up), as an example.

▪RSS feeds

Description: Syndicated information made available by Web sites in Rich Site Summary (or Really Simple Syndication) formats. Delivers information automatically to subscribers.

▪Rule

Description: A line which can be made in many different thicknesses, either with a pen, by machine, or with graphic tape.

▪Runaround

Description: Text that is typeset around an illustration.

▪Run-on-Printing

Description: Continuing to print past the number ordered.

▪Run In

Description: A proofreader's notation directing that an existing break (such as a paragraph) be ignored and the text continued without break as one paragraph.

▪Running Copy

Description: text, as opposed to headlines.

▪Running Heads

The book title or chapter title found at the top of the page in many books.

S

◊S3

Amazon's service that provides data storage infrastructure is referred to as the three S's. **S3** stands for **S**imple **S**torage **S**ervice. The advanced technology allows for retrieving any amount of data, at any time, from anywhere.

▪Saddle Stitching

Description: Binding a booklet or magazine by driving staples through the fold at the very center. Not practical for publications of more than seventy-two pages.

◊Sales Dashboard

Discussion: Amazon's Kindle Direct Publishing added a new Sales Dashboard in 2014, to the KDP Reports page to give up-to-date reporting of paid, borrowed and free orders as they are placed in Kindle stores worldwide. The new dashboard also helps track royalties earned as payments are processed for these orders. Authors link on the KDP Reports where they are given up-to-date reporting of paid, borrowed and free orders. The new dashboard also helps track royalties earned as payments are processed. Features continue to be added and improved. Currently objectives are:

1. Track orders as they are placed: The dashboard graph provides

daily trends for all titles as orders are placed in Kindle stores worldwide.

2. Track royalties as payments are processed: The dashboard displays a summary of royalties earned as payments are processed for orders.

3. Generate customized royalty reports: The downloadable report gives a detailed picture of orders, refunds and royalties earned and filter the Sales Dashboard and Sales & Royalty Report by title, marketplace, and timeframe. The information currently received in the Prior Six Weeks' Royalties reports is now available in the new Sales Dashboard and Sales & Royalty Report. That feature will eventually be removed.

▪Sales Handles

Description: Sales Handles are three or more specific points that explain a new book title's market place and why the book will do well. Sales handles convey what is new and different, the author's background and authority, the book's marketplace, its advantages over competition, and marketability. Most often, sales handles are combined with media angles (key points to convey to the media).

One approach in formulating descriptions is to ask yourself questions you'd like to be asked in an interview and figure great answers. Here's also a main target area; name three reasons the media should interview you. If you can name them, then you have come up with the handles and angles.

▪Sales Rep

Description: An individual who represents a publisher's books to retailers, wholesalers, etc., in exchange for a commission.

▪Sample Pages

Description: Typeset examples of a book's intended design.

▪SAN

SAN stands for Standard Account Number. Sometimes used in order fulfillment. A publisher's identification of book dealers, libraries, schools, and school system.

▪Scaling

Using a proportion wheel to size an illustration for printing. Scaling determines how much to enlarge or reduce a photograph.

○Schocken

Schocken Books, founded by Salman Schocken in Germany in 1931, began publishing in the United States in 1945 and became part of Random House, Inc., in 1987. Building upon its historic commitment to publishing Judaica, Schocken's authors include S. Y. Agnon, Sholem Aleichem, Aharon Appelfeld, Martin Buber, Tikva Frymer-Kensky, Franz Kafka, Francine Klagsbrun, Harold S. Kushner, Joan Nathan, Rabbi Jonathan Sacks, Gershom Scholem, Rabbi Adin Steinsaltz, Elie Wiesel, Simon Wiesenthal, and Dr. Avivah Zornberg.

▪Screen

Description: A masking device used to create various tints of the same color; 10 percent is very pale, 100 percent is the darkest tint possible.

▪Scribes

Description: People who were employed to copy text before the advent of printing technology.

○Scrivener

Scrivener is a word-processing software focusing on outlining, structuring, taking notes, and tracking sources.

▪Search and Replace

Description: A word processing function that automatically finds and replaces words or text throughout a document.

▪Search Engine

Description: The most popular way to find resources on the Internet. There are numerous search engines, each with a unique capability and style.

◊Search Inside The Book

Amazon Trademark; Search Inside!™ allows you to search millions of pages to find exactly the book you want to buy. With Search Inside!, search results will include titles based on every word inside the book. Search Inside! results are displayed interspersed with results that match the title and/or author of the book.

▪Second Serial Rights

Description: The rights for a magazine excerpt that will appear after the publication date.

▪Sector Expert

Description: An author who specialized in writing works on a certain topic or in a specific genre or field.

▪Self-Cover

Description: A cover consisting of the same paper stock as used for the inside pages.

▪Self-Publishing

Discussion: Authors who also publish their works are self-published. The author uses his or her own resources without the assistance of an established publisher to go through the process.

◊Sellers

Sellers is a slang term used by Amazon.com. The word was coined in 2000 when the web based business began to offer its best-of-breed e-commerce platform to other retailers and to individual sellers. Hundreds of thousands of world-class retail brands and individual sellers increase their sales and reach new customers by leveraging the power of the Amazon.com e-commerce platform. Partners work with *Amazon Services* to power their e-commerce offerings from end-to-end, including technology services, merchandising, customer service, and order fulfillment. Other branded merchants leverage Amazon.com as an incremental sales channel for their new merchandise. Amazon has teams across the world working on behalf of its customers at Fulfillment Centers, which provide fast, reliable shipping directly from Amazon's retail websites, and Customer Service Centers, which provide 24/7 support. In addition, Amazon's technology teams are located in Seattle and in International Development Centers designed to tap the world's best technical talent.

▪Sell Sheet

A sell sheet is basically a calling card to a company. It is used throughout all industries to show a company your products, books, and benefits. There is no one size fits all when it comes to sell sheets. The formatting can be anything. They can be very professional looking with graphs and illustrations or photographs. Sell sheets can be on high gloss paper or paper with a dull finish. The major point is to convey benefits in a short and concise manner on one or two pages of letter sized paper. The sell sheet is comparable to the blurb on the back of a novel, but with illustrations. Pick up a book and read the back. It gives a short overview of the book's storyline. Based on that blurb the Writer is hoping to peak interest, enough to buy it. The same can be said for the sell sheet. The format can get an idea in front of a company representative with the hopes they will read it, understand it, and see the book's potential.

A very good reason for using only two pages or less applies to the statement of getting a verbal pitch down to 30 seconds. It is all a matter of time. The person hearing the pitch or reading the sell sheet does not want to waste a lot of time trying to "Get" the idea. The quicker they "GET" the idea and understand it does a couple of things. One, if they "Get" the idea quickly and like it the presenter is much closer to gaining a licensing agreement.

The second is if they really like the idea and its usefulness they can also see that the public may "Get" the book's benefits, which means successful sales. No matter how good the contents may be if the company feels they'll have to educate the consumer before they "Get" the idea, they may pass on it. Depending on the (ROI) Return on Investment calculation the company will decide whether it is worth the cost of educating the public or it just isn't worth the time and investment. The sell sheet must put the author's best foot forward. It is best to ask the receiver if they have a compatible program before sending them the sell sheet attachment via e-mail. Specific guideline checklist...

1. Make sure your contact information is on every page.

2. Put your best short description of the products benefits.

3. Put your best short description of the products benefits.

4. Put your best short description of the products benefits.

5. Make sure any photos or illustrations are clear and give the best visuals.

6. Make sure a website is listed which shows other published books.

▪Serial

Description: A publication issued in successive parts, usually at regular intervals.

▪Serial Comma

Serial refers to the final comma in a sentence that lists items. Specifically, it is the comma immediately preceding the coordinating conjunction which helps avoid ambiguity.

◊Series

A book series is a sequence of books having certain characteristics in common that are formally identified together as a group. Book series can be organized in different ways, such as written by the same author, or marketed as a group by their publisher.

In Amazon.com, Series is accommodated by Clicking "This book is part of a series". There is an advantage because down the road a publisher/author will want to create more books related to the subject matter.

▪Series Title

Description: A part of the front matter of a book, when that book happens to be part of a larger series. Specifically, the part of the front matter that contains the title of the work, volume, the name of the general editor, and the titles of previous works in the series.

▪Seven Habits

Seven habits is an publishing industry slogan, a reminder that success comes from practicing correct habits. They are basically..

1. Own Your Niche
2. Select promotable authors and treat them right
3. Cultivate word of mouth
4. Make Things Easy
5. Ask for what you want
6. Apply the 80/20 rule
7. 7. Follow-up and follow-up again and again

○ShareAsImage.com

Description: A website that highlights text anywhere on the web and easily converts it into an image or can be customized to utilize and image with added text. The PRO version can choose fonts, colors and text size. Once created, the quote image can be shared on Pinterest, Facebook, or Twitter.

▪Sharing

Sharing on social-media websites is the act of posting links or material in a way that communicates it to friends, fans, followers, or other members in the network.

▪Sheetfed Press

Description: A press that requires paper cut into separate sheets, rather than a continuous roll. (sim. Web press)

◊Shelfari

Description: Amazon's online community of authors, publishers, and readers whose mission is to "enhance the experience of reading by connecting readers in meaningful conversations about the published word."

◊Shop with Points

Shop with Points offers customers the ability to pay for purchases at Amazon.com using credit card rewards points. Customers can use points to pay for an order at Amazon.com in the same way they would with any other method. Use rewards points to pay for part or all of a purchase, proceed to checkout through the Amazon.com Shopping Cart. Choose payment option for the purchase. Then choose the amount of points to apply. Points applied will be displayed in the Order Summary below the "Place Your Order" button. Shop with Points generally is available to buy millions of products at Amazon.com.

▪Short Discount

The term means less than 40%. Textbooks are often sold on a short discount (usually 20%).

▪Short Rated

Description: When advertising contract obligations are not met and the advertiser is rebilled at the higher actual usage rates.

▪Short Run

Description: A small printing job of a few hundred or a few thousand books or booklets.

▪Shrink-Wrapping

Description: A particular book cover option is called shrink-wrapping. If the cover isn't film-laminated, a clear plastic protection can be done. It is recommended if the cover has heavy ink coverage in a dark tone, or a very light colored background. That being the case, chances are the books will get scuffed during shipping. The additional process can be accomplished in lots of three or five and is generally inexpensive to do.

○SID shopper ID

Description: A method that enables a publisher to track where their referred actions originated, SID was started so they can target and/or reward their unique shoppers. When the visitor makes a purchase or completes a lead form, that transaction is tracked and recorded by Commission Junction (for example).

▪Signature

Description: A part of a book obtained by folding a large single sheet of paper into sections. A book signature may contain increments of 32 or 48 pages.

▪Signature Block

Description: Text that is automatically added to the end of an e-mail or forum post that usually contains the person's name and contact information.

▪Silk-Screening

Description: A printing method whereby ink is forced through a stencil, thus creating a design. It is a more expensive process used for imprinting heavy stock paper.

▪Simultaneous Editions

Simultaneous Editions is the printing of hardcover and paperback editions of a book at the same time (split run).

▪Sinkage

Description: The extra white space above a display, such as at a chapter opening.

▪Site License

A license to use a book or software within a facility that provides authorization to install the software on all or some number of servers for a specified number of users at specified locations as well as make copies of the book or software for distribution within that jurisdiction.

▪SKU

Stop-Keeping-Units (**SKU**) is a retail trade term used to identify particular items being sold. Use SKU to assist in the inventory automation systems. Assigned SKU's to each book or product can be numbers, letters, or a combination.

○**Skype**

Skype is an online service that enables users to make video calls and phone calls and send instant messages.

▪Slipcase

Description: A protective boxlike container, open at one end, for books.

▪Slippage

The term is used to denote lateness in a schedule, when a date slips because a partner in the production process (such as an external supplier, like an author, has not kept to the agreed dates and delivered on time.

▪Slug

Description: Spacing between lines of type wider than the usual two or three points of leading.

▪Small Caps

Description: A proofreader's direction (sc) to set material in uppercase letters the same size as the lowercase letters being used.

▪Smart Apostrophe

Definition: An apostrophe that is curled as opposed to a straight line type.

▪Smart Dash

Definition: A dash that is elongated to denote its specific meaning: em or en dash, for instance.

▪Smart Quotation Marks

Definition: A quotation mark that is curled in lieu of straight lines.

○Smashwords

Smashwords is an author-services company and distributor working on a fifteen percent commission. It is the world's largest distributor of indie e-books. The company claims they make it fast, free and easy for any author or publisher, anywhere in the world, to publish and distribute e-books to the major retailers (Apple, Barnes & Noble, Kobo, Sony, and Diesel; but not Amazon). Authors and publishers retain full control over how their works are published, sampled, priced and sold. If an author wants to give it away for free, they have that freedom.

▪Smyth Sewn

Description: Signatures sewn together with thread prior to installing the book cover is a common method with hardbound books.

▪Social Media

Description: A term describing interactive online platforms such as Google+, Facebook, Twitter, or LinkedIn allowing users to share posts, photos, and comments.

▪Social Network

Description: An online community of people who discuss common interests.

▪Soft Cover

Description: A book bound in a flexible paper cover and sold at a lower price than a hardcover book.

○SPAN

SPAN stands for Small Publishers Association of North America which is a nonprofit trade association for authors, self-publishers, and independent presses.

○SPD

The Standard Periodical Directory (SPD) is an essential reference work that lists more than seventy-five thousand North American periodicals. Published since 1964, the 2000-page book is the largest directory with information on more than 60,000 magazines, journals, newsletters, newspapers, and directories. The source is indispensable to libraries, researchers, marketers, printers, publishers, ad agencies, promotion specialists, and anyone who needs to know which publications are covering which fields.

▪Specs

Description: An abbreviation for specification, it means the physical details of a publishing project including type style, type size, binding, trim size, and page count.

▪Special Characters

Description: Symbols, punctuation marks, and other characters that are neither numbers nor letters such as @#$%^&.

▪Special Standard Rate

Description: Successor to *book rate* and now called Media mail.

▪Spell Out

Description: (sp) is a proofreader's mark meaning to spell out, rather than abbreviate or use initials.

▪Spine

A part of a book to which the pages are attached and on the outside where there usually appears the book title and author's name, and sometimes the publisher's name and logo.

▪Spine Out

The term is a directive to display books on a shelf so that the spine information shows and not face-out.

▪Spiral Binding

Definition: Continuous wire binding, also referred to as coil binding. The Spiral Binding Company Inc. are the creators of Spiral Binding.

▪SRDS

SRDS stands for Standard rate and Data Services, Inc. Published reference books are designed especially for ad agencies but useful in other marketing efforts too.

▪Stet

Definition: A proofreading term to disregard editing notes and leave as is. From the Latin "to stand."

▪Stitch

Description: A staple. The staples seen in magazines and brochures are "saddle stitches."

▪STOP Orders

Description: A cash with order (Single Title Order Plan) used by bookstores.

▪Strike-on-Type

Description: Cold type created with a typewriter, composer or computer character printer where the typeface makes an impression on paper through a carbon ribbon.

▪Strip In

Definition: To combine a photograph negative with one or more others in preparation for making a printing plate.

▪Stripping

Description: The process of preparing a negative or series of negatives for plate making.

○StumbleUpon

The online community of people who stumble upon websites and rate them. In so doing, they enter the websites into the StumbleUpon system for the rest of the community.

○Styles

The Microsoft Word feature is in the Format menu of Microsoft Word. It is designed to let users apply various sets of formatting choices to paragraphs.

Style Sheet

Description: A guide to editorial specifications, or selected typographical details, for a particular book.

Stylebook

Description: Also called a handbook of style, this references The Chicago Style, as one example and intended to ensure consistency within, and correct handling of, written works.

Subhead

Definition: A heading within a chapter that identifies and separates topics within that chapter.

Subsidiary Rights

Definition: Additional rights to publish the book in other forms. Examples are book club rights, foreign rights and serial rights.

Subsidy Press

Description: A publisher who charges the author to publish a book. Subsidy presses have a bad reputation for editing, production and promotion (vanity press).

Substantive Editing

Definition: Extensive changes to a manuscript to adjust flow and organization and to refine word choices and phrasing.

▪Subtitle

Description: A second or additional title further explaining a nonfiction book's content and scope.

▪Syndication

Definition: The simultaneous release of written or broadcast material to many outlets.

○SXSW Interactive

Description: The annual conference in Austin, Texas, focusing on emerging technologies and new media.

11 T-U

T

▪Table of Contents

Description: A section in the front matter of a book where its various chapters and subheadings are listed along with their page number locations.

▪Table of Illustrations

Description: A section in the front matter noting illustrations used in the text and their page numbers.

▪Tablet

Description: An industry coined term referencing a personal computer type that has a touchscreen and can be operated with fingertips, a stylus, or both. This is a popular ebook reader as well.

◊Tags

Discussion: Amazon Tags feature has been discontinued; however, all the tags previously created are still available under the author's Profile page. Originally, the Tags feature was to allow customers to tag items they were considering to purchase, tagging products and books that they previously purchased for later recommendations, and tagging products to suggest better organization of them for Amazon. Over time Amazon has introduced new features which have replaced the Tags functionality, so you may be interested in learning more about features such as Wish Lists, Customer Reviews, and Recommendations.

▪Tags

Discussion: Authors use words when dialogue is in-play. A tag is said or asked. The point of a tag is basically to let the reader know who's saying what. Professional writers claim it best to avoid creativity in tags. When words like hiss, growl, beg, and demand are used, the industry's show, don't tell principle is revealed; a sign of weak dialogue. Here's a good example. The original line used is, "Go home now," he demanded. An improvement would be, "She doesn't want you living here." Jim shoved him out the door. "Go back home where you belong."

▪Tailpiece

Description: A type of label users can assign to online content to categorize, sort, and search information.

○Tales from the Reading Room

Wordpress.com has this section available which claims this to be "A Literary Salon Where All Are Welcome." Go to

http://litlove.wordpress.com/

▪Target Audience

Description: A process of determining specialized advertising. A small publisher competes with the biggies and will look like a mouse in the shadow of a lion unless you identify a specific core audience. That's why niche books that appeal to a particular group because the sphere of influence is limited.

▪Technical Editing

Description: The process of making corrections and revisions to a book about a technical subject, both for technical errors and errors involving language usage (grammar and spelling).

▪Tear Sheets

Description: Ads, stories, etc., torn from the magazine they appeared in.

▪Terms

Definition: The specified number of days a customer is allowed before paying, as in "net 30."

○TED

TED stands for Technology, Entertainment and Design. Annual events define its mission as "ideas worth spreading" where the collection of conferences features highly qualified speakers who discuss their passions and expertise.

○TED Books

TED Books are shorter than a novel, but longer than a magazine article. The books are short original electronic books produced by TED Conferences. Like the best TED Talks, they're personal and provocative, and designed to spread great ideas. Books are typically under 20,000 words — long enough to unleash a powerful narrative, but short enough to be read in a single sitting.

○Three Day Novel Contest

The 3-Day Novel Contest is administered by the Geist Foundation in Vancouver, along with the generous help of numerous volunteer judges and supporters from the writing, publishing and arts communities. Visit the Contest History page to read about the organizations that began and nurtured this unique literary institution. - See more at:

http://www.3daynovel.com/about/#sthash.lK9XOp6A.dpuf

◊Thomas & Mercer

Description: An imprint of Amazon Publishing specializing in mysteries and thrillers.

▪TIFF

Description: A standard image file format commonly used by publishers for cover and interior images.

▪Time to Market

Description: An industry standard term referring to the time between a manuscript completion and when the final book becomes available for consumer purchase.

▪Tipping In

Definition: The pasting into a book of extra sheets such as foldout maps.

▪Title Page

Description: The page in the front matter of a book that contains the full title of the work, the subtitle, the name of the author, and the name and location of the publisher.

▪TLC

Description: The recognizable symbol standing for trustworthiness, likeability, and competence; the three pillars of establishing an enchanting personal brand.

▪Tour

Discussion: Book tours provide much value. Getting that little bit of time with the author— the face time—really keeps people's interest. Face it, when people go to the bookstores, there are a million books. Author appearances draw people to the author. Usually a publicist prepares and sends the itinerary to the showcase author a day before the tour. Careful planning and follow-up is essential since one big and common problem is when the booksellers do not stock up on extra book copies in anticipation of local media interviews.

▪Track Links

Description; Booksellers, wholesalers, and authors Track by using a website called BITLY. http://www.bitly.com

▪Trade Book

A Trade book is a title intended for general readership, as opposed to academic or technical use.

▪Trade Paperback

A Trade Paperback simply refers to a top quality paperback (in lieu of inexpensive throughways).

▪Trade Industry

Description: Booksellers, wholesalers, business organizations, schools, and libraries belong to the publishing exchange applied to international trade.

▪Trade Publishers' Approach

Description: A purposeful advertising method that the major publishers use. Target Audiences are the trade industry, consumers, and subsidiaries all to impress agents, authors, and create a positive *house* image.

▪Traditional PR

Description: Publicity methods other than social-media marketing, especially those relying on older approaches such as reaching out to major news outlets.

▪Traditional Publishing

Description: The alternative to self-publishing, and the process of publishing works through major publishing houses such as Penguin and Harper-Collins.

○Trafford

Description: An author-services imprint of Author Solutions.

▪Transfer Type

Description: The sheets of characters, numerals, borders or symbols that may be burnished onto paper and added to the paste-up.

▪Traveler

Description: The book traveler is a sales representative.

○TrialPay

Description: One payment method that customers can use on E-Junkie, PayPal, Authorize.net, and Google Checkout.

○Tumblr

Description: One of the four major blogging platforms, along with Blogger, TypePad, and WordPress. Authors can tell their story through pictures, animation, text, music, video, and more in this state-of-the art multimedia content stream.

○Twain

Discussion: For Your Image Capture Web App. TWAIN has been around since 1992. The TWAIN Working Group, which represents the imaging industry, put together the TWAIN standard. Many technology vendors in the imaging space make up the group. As the working group puts it, the purpose of TWAIN is "to provide and foster a universal public standard which links applications and image acquisition devices." As a result, today we have the TWAIN standard. It is a software protocol and applications programming interface (API) that regulates communication between software applications and imaging devices. This article will touch upon the history of TWAIN and its wide use before diving into developer planning considerations. With a focus on developing image capturing applications to use within web-based document management applications, the article will uncover 8 rules for TWAIN-based application development. If you've used an imaging device to scan something, chances are you've come across TWAIN somewhere in the scanning software. Using the TWAIN standard to scan something has been made quite simple over the years. But, developing web applications to leverage the standard is not so easily done. Web application developers must consider several factors before embarking on such a task. Software and web app developers have long used TWAIN to link their applications with imaging devices. Today, this link is more critical than ever. Industries such as healthcare, financial use of TWAIN will only grow. In fact, many companies – from small businesses to large publicly-traded technology vendors – use TWAIN in their document management solutions. And, vendors sell these solutions into healthcare, financial, government and other such industries. The use of image capturing within document management applications has many advantages. There's a reduction in paper costs, a streamlining of workflow processes, simpler collaboration, enhanced security possibilities, and more. So, as web application developers continue to leverage TWAIN more and more, what are the critical elements to consider?and government largely use document management solutions for their paper-heavy industries. As more organizations move from a paper-based process to digital document management, the importance and

○**Tweet**

Discussion: Inside a Tweet there are photos and videos from familiar people or behind-the-scenes moments from the biggest stars. Users link to news stories, blogs, websites and apps.

Twitter was born as a mobile service. It was designed to fit into the character limit of a text message, and Twitter still works on any SMS-ready phone. Brevity keeps Twitter fast-paced and relevant by encouraging people to Tweet in the moment and to focus on the essential idea they are trying to communicate.

Once a user Tweets, it is publicly posted on their Twitter profile. In addition, people can follow their stream of Tweets called a timeline so that they automatically appear in their own timelines.

To post a Tweet via the web:

1. Sign in to your Twitter account.

2. Type your Tweet into the box on the left side of your screen, or click the compose new Tweet button in the top navigation bar. It looks like this:

3. Make sure your update is fewer than 140 characters. We'll count the

characters for you! Remaining characters show up as a number below the box.

4. Click the Tweet button to post the Tweet to your profile.

5. You will immediately see your Tweet in the timeline on your homepage. Once you Tweet, it is publicly posted on your Twitter profile. In addition, people can follow your stream of Tweets called a timeline so that they automatically appear in their own timelines.

To post a Tweet via text message (SMS): Another way (some say the best way!) to post updates is from your mobile phone. First, connect your phone with your Twitter account, then simply send your Tweet as a text message to your appropriate Twitter short code the same way you'd send any other text message. Remember to count your characters! To delete a Tweet:

1. To delete a Tweet that you have posted, please read this article.

2. Note that you can only delete Tweets which you posted yourself from your account.

3. You cannot delete Tweets which were posted by other accounts. Instead, you can unfollow or block users whose tweets you do not want to receive.

4. If you are trying to delete a retweet you can read this article to learn more about undo a retweet.

Subscribing to someone's stream of Tweets is called "following". To start following someone, click the Follow button next to their name, and you'll see their Tweets as soon as they post something new.

Start by following people you know. Search for their names or their @handles or find them all instantly by importing your contacts. Then look for your favorite sports teams, actors, local newspapers, writers or schools. Lastly, look for accounts of people sending the type of Tweets you'd like to receive: breaking news, celebrity gossip or professional updates.

You don't have to ask permission to follow someone. Anyone on Twitter can follow or unfollow anyone else at any time. This leads to something unexpected: open and fun conversations that get people talking.

A private message (sometimes called a DM or direct message) is a private Tweet between two people who follow each other. To read your messages, click on the envelope icon on your profile.

Your profile is where you show people what they can expect from your Tweets and why they should follow you. Add a photo, short description and background image to give the world a taste of your personality.

○**T**weetdeck

Description: A standalone software application for Twitter featuring a multi-column orientation.

◊**T**wenty Thousand (20,000) Rule

Discussion: Successful Kindle Store authors pick a niche where at least three books get this sales volume. Generally, it is a rule of thumb or a quick litmus test for a sales market which numbers about five book sales a day. So figures include an average $2.99 price with a $2 profit per book which equates to about $3,650 annually. This is certainly not an exact science, but experts agree that it is important to look closely at a targeted market where actual people on Amazon buy products on this particular popular topic.

○Twitter

Description: A major social networking website that revolves around 140-character messages called tweets. Users can send these messages to their followers, or follow other users like friends, celebrities, favorite brands, and so on to receive those messages.

■Two Up

Description: Pieces printed side by side.

■Typeface

Description: The style of the letter or character of the type.

■TypePad

Description: One of the four major blogging platforms along with Blogger, Tumblr, and WordPress. Six Apart, the parent company of TypePad sold to VideoEgg – creating a new organization known as Say Media. TypePad currently serves a niche and fits nicely between a continuum ranging from microblog platforms such as Tumblr and Posterious on the one side, and the more robust WordPress platform on the other.

■Typesetter

Description: A typesetter does *typesetting* which is the composition of text by means of types. Stored letters and other symbols (called sorts in mechanical systems and glyphs in digital systems) are retrieved and ordered according to a language's orthography for visual display. Typesetting requires the prior process of designing a font. Computers excel at automatically typesetting and correcting documents.

Character-by-character, computer-aided phototypesetting was, in turn, rapidly rendered obsolete in the 1980s by fully digital systems employing a raster image processor to render an entire page to a single high-resolution digital image, now known as image setting.

U

▪UCC

UCC means Universal Copyright Convention which is an agreement, ratified by ninety nations, to offer the copyrighted works of citizens of other nations the same protections as are extended to those of their own citizens.

▪Unbound

Definition: A crowdfunding website dedicated to books.

▪URL

URL is the abbreviation for Uniform Resource Locator which is the full name and address of a web site.

▪UPC

UPC is the abbreviation for Universal Product Code used to identify a manufactured item.

○UIPD

Description: Ulrich's International Periodicals Directory (UIPD) offers an excellent source of magazines of the entire world. The directory is broken down by subject and cross-referenced. It also notes which periodicals have regular book reviews posted. It is now supplied on-line as Ulrichsweb, which provides web-based and Z39.50 linking to library catalogs. The online version includes over 300,000 active and current periodicals.

▪Underrun

Definition: When a printer manufactures fewer copies than ordered.

▪Unit Cost

Definition: The cost to print each book.

▪Universal Copyright Convention

Description: An agreement, ratified by ninety nations, to offer the copyrighted works of citizens of other nations the same protections as are extended to those of their own citizens.

▪Universal Discount Schedule

Description: A system that gives everyone the same discounts, whether wholesaler, bookstore, individual, or library.

▪Up-Charge

Description: An additional fee incurred over and above a stated price.

▪User-Generated Reviews

Description: User-generated reviews are created by ordinary users and book readers, as opposed to those professionally created.

▪URL

URL stands for Uniform Resource Locator. The full name (address) of a Web site, such as www.SelPublishingResources.com

▪Utilities

Description: Tools for writers to back up manuscripts, store tidbits of information, and transfer large files.

▪UV Coating

Description: Liquid applied to a printed sheet, then bonded and cured with ultraviolet light.

12 V-W-X-Y-Z

V

▪Value Statement

This industry term describes the basic foundation for effective book marketing. Author statements must be compelling or promotional efforts are wasted. Value statements describe a result that a book creates for people. A starting sentence should begin, "I will help you—." Avoid actions that steal the thunder such as...

a. Ambiguous phrases (not specific enough to draw attention).

b. Teaching points (causes guilt or embarrassment)

c. Technical terms or religious quotes

d. Negative statements

▪Vanity Publishing

Discussion: The term has a derogatory connotation because it implies that authors self-publish only after being rejected by mainstream publishers. Vanity publishing (or subsidy-publishing) is where an author pays (an exorbitant price to) a publisher to turn his or her manuscript into a book. Subsidy publishers offer production services like editing and cover design that make them attractive to writers who want one-stop shopping. Their rough manuscript is turned into a book and made available through major book distribution channels. Basically, an author pays someone to be their publisher (hence the term *subsidy publishing*). The bait and switch happens when the title becomes part of the publisher's catalog. Subsidy publishers assign an ISBN number that belongs to *them; they* become the publisher of record which entitles *them* to receive an additional royalty whenever a book sells. Charging for editing, design, and production services is perfectly acceptable, but charging an additional publisher's royalty is unethical unless they've taken some risk. Also, the publisher sets the book's retail price so the book is usually priced higher than the market.

▪Varnishing

Description: A coating process that results in a hard, glossy surface. Used for protection and eye appeal on book covers.

◊Velocity Limits

Discussion: As a means of protecting customers, Amazon monitors "sales velocity" - the number and dollar amount of a seller's transactions during any given month. When a seller approaches or exceeds Amazon's current velocity limit, the account is evaluated and the velocity limit may be adjusted. Sellers do not need to contact Amazon to have the velocity limit augmented. Increases are granted or denied as part of a strict proactive evaluation. During the evaluation, new orders may appear as "pending".

Thus, orders will not have "confirm" or "cancel" buttons in the *Manage Orders*, and will not appear in either the Order Report or the Unshipped Orders Report which are not in a shippable status, and should not be shipped.

▪Vendor

Definition: A supplier of goods or services.

◊Verified Purchase

Discussion: A product or book review is marked "Amazon Verified Purchase," which means the customer who wrote the review purchased the item at Amazon.com. Customers can add this label to their review only if Amazon can verify the item being reviewed was purchased. Customers reading an Amazon Verified Purchase review can use this information to help them decide which reviews are most helpful in their purchasing decisions. If a review is not marked Amazon Verified Purchase, it doesn't mean that the reviewer has no reading experience with the book – it just means Amazon couldn't verify that it had been purchased. They may have purchased the item elsewhere or had some other interaction. If Amazon could somehow validate their experience, they certainly would. The Amazon Verified Review label offers one more way to help gauge the quality and relevance of a review. When someone writes a new review, they will be given the opportunity to mark the review as an Amazon Verified Purchase. If the checkbox doesn't appear, Amazon wasn't able to verify purchase. If someone writes a review for an item they purchased at Amazon previously and would like to mark it as an Amazon Verified Purchase, they simply edit the existing review and the Amazon Verified Purchase checkbox should appear. After checking the box and saving the review, the review will immediately be marked as an Amazon Verified Purchase.

▪Version Control

Description: The tracking and storing of drafts of a project over various stages of its creation in order to allow backtracking or the revisiting of older versions for reference.

▪Verso

Definition: Verso refers to a left-hand page, as opposed to a recto or right-hand page.

○Vintage Books

Discussion: Vintage Books was founded in 1954 by Alfred A. Knopf as a trade paperback home to its authors. Its publishing list includes a wide range, from the most influential works of world literature to cutting edge contemporary fiction and distinguished non-fiction. As the continuous publisher of important writers including William Faulkner, Vladimir Nabokov, Albert Camus, Ralph Ellison, Dashiell Hammett, William Styron, A.S. Byatt, Philip Roth, Toni Morrison, Ha Jin, Richard Ford, Cormac McCarthy, Alice Munro, Raymond Chandler, Orhan Pamuk, Dave Eggers, Robert Caro, Joseph Ellis, Haruki Murakami, and Gabriel Garcia Marquez it is today's foremost trade paperback publisher.

○Vintage Español

Description: This division of Random House, Inc., was founded in 1994 as a distinguished group by Alfred A. Knopf in an effort to publish selected works of fiction and nonfiction in Spanish. Since then, it has expanded to become one of the largest Spanish-language publishers in the United States, offering a growing list of titles across a wide variety of genres, including, in addition to fiction and nonfiction, sports, spirituality, self-help, personal finance and cooking, to name a few. Our authors include Gabriel García Márquez, Roberto Bolaño, Ken Follett, Isabel Allende, Junot Diaz, Dr. Isabel Gomez-Bassols, Jorge Amado and Cristina Garcia, among many others.

Viral Marketing

Description: Viral Marketing is a word-of-mouth promotion, especially on the internet. It involves placing promotional information in a system community, where those who read it pass it on to others, thus themselves contributing to the marketing process.

Virtual Book Tour

Description: A book tour conducted through electronic media, such as guest appearances on blogs or podcasts.

Virtual Staff Finder

Discussion: A book business grows and necessitates time saving measures. A team is usually built around this online business. Authors will find that the best way to spend their new income is to reinvest into what works well. A full time virtual assistant which can be done through (http://www.VirtualStaffFinder.com/) will handle a great deal of repetitive tasks.

▪Vlog

Description: A blog that has video content as well as text.

▪VOR

VOR stands for Vendor of Record. A term used by distributors and wholesalers to designate one company as the primary source for book returns.

○ **W**attpad

Definition: An online community, primarily for writers and readers of novels and poetry, that focuses on feedback and collaboration.

■ **W**eb 2.0

Description: The term associated with a range of technologies encompassing information sharing, collaboration, and development on the Web, including communities, hosted services, applications, social networking sites, video sharing sites, etc. the term was originally coined by Tim O'Reilly, CEO and founder of O'Reilly Media, in 2004.

■ **W**eb Press

Web Press is a fast, sophisticated printing press that uses roll-fed paper rather than sheets (also *Sheetfed* Press).

■ **W**eb Services

Web Services is a cloud computing platform that started as a way to keep track of orders. Now it is an industry service, a method of communicating between two electronic devices over the World Wide Web. Technically it is a software function in conjunction with a network address over the web. The service can always on as in the concept of utility computing.

○ **W**hat the Plus

Description: The Google+ guide for self-publishing the first attempt.

■**W**holesaler

Description: A business that buys books in quantities for resale to stores and libraries. Wholesalers handle all or most books, do not usually have sales reps and are not exclusive to special markets; not a distributor.

■**W**holesale Price

Definition: The price paid for a book or product initially when sold to a reseller, as opposed to retail or final consumer price.

○ **W**ho's Who in U.S. Writers, Editors and Poets

The December Press published Who's Who in U.S. Writers, Editors and Poets in 1993. The book is outdated but can still be purchased *used* from Amazon.com.

◊**W**hispersync

Description: Optional read and audible, Voice lets you enjoy more books, more often. But even better, the convenience of being able to switch between professional narration and reading enriches the reader's experience.

▪Widget

Description: A small piece of prebuilt, self-contained code that can be easily embedded in existing applications or websites.

○Widget

Description: The (iBooks Author) small interactive components used in Apple's Multi-Touch iBooks providing a rich media experience.

▪Widow

Description: A hallmark of poor page layout. A widow is when the last line of a paragraph appears by itself on the following page or in the next column; thus separated from the rest of the text.

○Wikipedia

Description: A multilingual, web-based, free-content encyclopedia project operated by the Wikimedia Foundation and based on an openly editable model.

◊Wish List

Discussion: Amazon Convenience that Keeps track of what someone wants. Also, it is now possible to add items from other websites to an Amazon Wish List: Under a book or product, two buttons are labeled. One says, 'Add to Wish List', the other is 'Add to Cart'. Users can create a Wish List profile and add items to their registry to keep track of the items they're eyeing. This is a strategy to boost a book's ranking by getting it added to the list. Simply activate the button on the book's page that says "Add To Wish List". Click on it to initiate. This is a way for general customers to add products to a list of what they'd like to purchase. When people add books it tells Amazon that a book is popular and people want it. This boosts a book's ranking.

User instructions are simple. Hover over Wish List at the top of any Amazon.com page and select Create a Wish List from the drop-down. (If you're creating multiple Wish Lists, go to an existing Wish List and click Create another Wish List under a profile name). Click - **Create your Wish List**. The Wish List will be available. Its name can be revised by hovering over the list name and clicking the Edit list name link. Finally, select Edit list profile from the List Actions filter at the top of this list to update any default shipping address, birthday, personal description and preferences. This information can be updated again anytime. Click Save and browse for an item. Click Add to Wish List under the Buy box on the right-hand side of any item's product detail page. Repeat this process to create multiple Wish Lists; there's no limit. A default Wish List is the one where items are added when clicking Add to Wish List.

○ **W**iki

Description: A **wiki** is a web application which invites users to edit any page or to create new pages, using only a plain-vanilla Web browser without any extra add-ons. For example, the encyclopedia project Wikipedia is the most popular wiki on the public web. Anyone can add, modify, or delete content in collaboration with others. In a typical wiki, text is written using a simplified markup language or a rich-text editor. While a wiki is a type of content management system, it differs from a blog or most other such systems in that the content is created without any defined owner or leader, and wikis have little implicit structure, allowing structure to emerge according to the needs of the users.

Wikis can serve many different purposes both public and private, including knowledge management, note taking, community websites and intranets. Some permit control over different functions (levels of access). For example, editing rights may permit changing, adding or removing material. Others may permit access without enforcing access control. Other rules may also be imposed to organize content.

Ward Cunningham, the developer of the first wiki software, WikiWikiWeb, originally described it as "the simplest online database that could possibly work".

▪Window

Description: A sheet of red, orange or black paper or acetate on a paste-up, to indicate where a photograph will be positioned. These colors photograph as black, creating a clear "window" in the black negative.

○Wordclay

Description: An author-services imprint of Author Solutions.

▪Word of Mouth

Description: An informal but important kind of advertising in which a book is praised by one person to another.

○ WordPress

One of the four major blogging platforms, along with Blogger, Tumblr, and TypePad. There is no blogging platform without controversy. Wordpress has had plenty of issues with downtime and viruses, unfortunately.

■ Word Processor

Description: A software program producing typewritten documents with automated and usually computerized typing and text-editing equipment.

■ Work Made for Hire

Description: Work done for a fee in which the author has no copyright or ownership rights. Current law states the agreement must be in writing.

■ Working Title

Definition: The preliminary title used during manuscript preparation before the book is named.

○ WPN

The Working Press of the Nation (**WPN**) offers a comprehensive rundown of names and addresses and is user-friendly. The three-volume directory covers newspapers, magazines, and Internet publications, plus radio and television. Authors and publishers benefit by tapping into a list covering the important reviewers in both print and electronic media who would typically be interested in a new title. This is also an ideal place to prospect for syndicated columnists, as they are cross-referenced by subject area.

W3C

The World Wide Web Consortium (**W3C**) is the main international standards organization for the World Wide Web (abbreviated WWW or W3). The consortium is made up of member organizations which maintain full-time staff for the purpose of working together in the development of standards for the World Wide Web.

Writer's Cafe

WritersCafe.org is an online community where writers can post their work, get reviews, and connect with other writers.

Writers' Conference

Description: A networking event where writers go to meet agents, editors, and other writers.

Writer's Market

Description: A comprehensive annual compilation of publishers' and periodicals' names, addresses, current needs, and general policies and contract terms. This submission tracker website is essential for authors who want to investigate channels for distributing their manuscripts. (http://www.writersmarket.com)

Writers Store

The website is considered the ultimate resource for writing and filmmaking. The store supplies authors with software, books, supplies, courses, contests, services, and advice.

(http://www.writersstore.com)

○ **W**riting Software

There are several available; the following is a partial list.

1. **Character Writer**: Software that is considered the next generation of writing software, combining the power of the Enneagram personality-typing system and the latest technology. Character Writer is a cross-platform software package that offers both character-generating and story-generating tools in one easy-to-use interface. (www.characterpro.com)

2. **Contour**: This software is a proven story development system that streamlines the process of turning a movie idea from first glimmer to full outline. Using the Contour story development system created by Emmy Award-nominated Jeffrey Alan Schechter, learn how to use the same character-based structure that nearly all the blockbuster movies use to create solid stories that hold together from Fade In to Fade Out. With its intuitive, fill-in-the-blanks approach, Contour shows you exactly what elements need to be in a script, never again leaving you to wonder, "what comes next?" A must-have for every screenwriter. (www.marinersoftware.com)

3. **Power Writer**: Power Writer allows you to create anything from a short story all the way up to a full novel in one powerful, easy-to-use program. It fully integrates outlining and story development tools so that your writing can proceed as one continuous act of creation from first idea through finished manuscript. (http://www.writersstore.com/power-writer-novel-writing-software/)

4. **Truby's Genre**: The software is the only screenwriting program of its kind to focus on writing for specific genres. With add-ons for action, comedy, horror and every genre of screenwriting, Blockbuster can be tailored to fit exactly the style of movie you're working on. (http://www.writersstore.com/trubys-blockbuster-genre-add-on/)

5. **Trudy's Blockbuster**: The program puts hundreds of professional techniques at your fingertips to help create a great story, in a fraction of the usual time and effort. Based on an interface that teaches as you write, Blockbuster shows you the deep structural weaknesses that are likely to be in your script and takes you through the ideal order for fixing them. (http://www.writersstore.com/trubys-blockbuster-screenplay-structure-software/)

6. **Contour**: As a proven story development writing software, the program streamlines the process of turning movie ideas from first glimmer to full outline. Using Contour software and its story developer, you'll learn how to apply the same character-based structure that nearly all blockbuster movies use to create solid stories that hold together from Fade In to Fade Out. (http://contour.com/pages/storyteller)

7. **The Cut'N'Mix Word Machine**: The Cut'n'Mix application helps creative writers generate new ideas through the use of different methods of text randomization and manipulation. Cut'n'Mix expands the palette of tools available to writers, with functions not available in standard word processors. (www.cutnmix.com)

8. **Character Pro**: Professional writers, actors and directors know that creating compelling characters is critical to great storytelling. Yet it's one of the hardest things to pull off. Character Pro provides a dedicated environment for focusing all your creative energy on developing the characters that will

bring your stories to life.
(http://www.characterpro.com/characterwriter/index.html)

9. **Storybase**: A sure-fire cure for writer's block, the program sparks imagination with thousands of narrative writing prompts, each suggesting multiple story possibilities. Plug in character information, and see dozens of conflict-based suggestions for scenes, relationships and motivation.
(http://storybase.software.informer.com/2.0/)

10. **Writer's Blocks**: No matter what you are writing, it can be challenging to keep track of all of your ideas, research, plot points, etc. This program frees you from working in a constricted linear way as you enter each idea into a moveable block...a Writer's Block. Now organizing your writing is as easy as dragging and dropping. Your blocks are all visible in your desktop, nothing is hidden. Zoom in to focus on one idea, or zoom out to get the big picture.
(http://www.writersblocks.com/)

11. **Great Dialogue Software**:™ The program has a database of thousands of samples of the best dialogue from movies, TV, novels and plays, all available at the click of a button. Just type in the subject matter of your scene and click "Find." Most of these samples have a detailed analysis to instruct you how the dialogue was constructed, the technique used, and why it works.
(http://www.greatdialogue.com/Doc_Help.htm)

12. **Idea Tracker**: The software offers an easy, customizable and effective method to organize, sort, filter, and print ideas, thoughts and/or notes. (www.intellectusenterprises.com)

13. **StoryCraft**: The program is a story-processing type--designed specifically for writing and completing any kinds of stories (from short stories to screenplays and novels)--that comes with

history's greatest writing coaches built right into it.
(www.writerspage.com)

14. **StoryMill**: From inception to sale, the program unlocks the secrets that get stories published. Part word processor, part database, and introducing an industry-first timeline feature that will interactively display a story across time, StoryMill empowers every author with the tools essential to writing a best seller. (www.marinersoftware.com)

15. **Final Draft**: Screenwriting software for script writing, including movie screenplays, TV scripts and stage plays; Puts your words into screenplay format as you type, Contains professional tools to help you learn how to write a screenplay. (http://store.finaldraft.com/)

16. **Persona**: The program is based on this concept: by categorizing characters into archetypes, you can know their background, which in turn shows their motivations, and then allows you to predict their behavior. To put it bluntly, it is the difference between deliberately crafting a compelling character or hoping that the character turns out the way you wanted. (https://marinersoftware.com/products/persona/)

17. **Dramatica Story Expert**: This software includes classic tools, like its outstanding question and answer system, and gives them a major overhaul while also adding tons of fresh features. From the completely new project overview window and optional icon toolbar to the revamped menus and enhanced StoryGuide and Master Story Engine windows, Dramatica Story Expert goes a long way toward making the story development process easier and more enjoyable. (http://www.dramaticastoryexpert.com/whats-new.html)

18. **MasterWriter**: Why struggle to find the right word or phrase, when you can have all the possibilities in an instant? MasterWriter is an unlimited source of ideas pre-inspiration, and an invaluable tool during the creative process. Its most important role may be post-inspiration, when finding a better way to express yourself or a more creative way to describe something, can be the difference between good and great. (http://www.masterwriter.com/)

19. **StyleWriter**: This software is the world's most powerful editor. It plugs directly into all versions of Microsoft Word, Word Perfect or any Windows application through the Clipboard. StyleWriter searches for thousands of writing faults, including complex words, jargon and abstract words, wordy phrases, hidden verbs, passive verbs, clichés and long sentences. It then pops up advice showing you how to edit each sentence. Using StyleWriter typically cuts 25 percent of the words from the document. (www.stylewriter-usa.com)

20. **Scrivener**: This word processor and project management tool was created specifically for writers of long texts such as novels and research papers. It won't try to tell you how to write - it just makes all the tools you have scattered around your desk available in one application. (https://www.literatureandlatte.com/trial.php)

21. **Writers-Support-Center**: Since 2004, WritersSuperCenter.com has provided writers with software for every writing purpose, from story-writing to article and essay writing to book writing and editing. Also distribute, through its StyleWriterForGovernment.com website, the StyleWriter Plain English Software, for improving the writing of businesses, organizations, and individuals, as well as government offices and agencies. (www.writerssupercenter.com,www.StyleWriterForGovernment.com)

▪<u>**W**rong Font</u>

Description: (wf) is used by a proofreader indicating that in one or more words, the printer used the wrong font (face) or type.

X

○**Xlibris**

Xlibris is an author-services imprint of Author Solutions.

▪**XML**

XML stands for Extensible Markup Language which lets web developers create customized tags for presenting electronic information.

Y

○ **YouSendIt**

An online service providing a way to transfer large files.

○ **YouTube**

A website letting people discover, watch, and share originally created videos.

Z

○**Z39.50**

Z39.50 is an international standard client–server, communications application protocol for searching and retrieving information from a database over a computer network. The industry term is derived by ANSI/NISO standard Z39.50, and ISO standard 23950. The standard's maintenance agency is the Library of Congress and widely used in library environments and incorporated into personal bibliographic reference software. Interlibrary catalogue searches are often implemented with Z39.50 queries. Work on the protocol began in the 1970s, and led to successive versions in 1988, 1992, 1995 and 2003. The Contextual Query Language (formerly called the Common Query Language) is based on Z39.50 semantics.

○**Z39** Standard

American National Standards Committee (ANSC) uses this nomenclature for measuring standards for libraries, information science and publishing.

○**Zappos**

Description: An online retailer of beauty products run by Amazon.com.

▪<u>ZIP</u>

Description: A file containing one or more files that have been compressed into the ZIP format, which saves computer storage space.

If you like this reference and find it very helpful, please post comments on the Amazon Review for this book. That way, others will be encouraged to read and learn important industry savvy and expressions. Since there are no other terminology sources for new writers and publishers, this initial edition will certainly be scrutinized, criticized, and challenged in many ways. It is difficult to keep up with all the changes taking place and a book like this needs constant upgrading. Your input, including additional words, phrases, and helpful consulting businesses, will assist in this endeavor.

Review suggestions, both positive and negative, will certainly be appreciated. If interest grows in this arena of ideas, look for more terms, added information, industry term clarifications, new support companies, more explanations, recommendations, and upgrades.

CADARM PUBLICATIONS
OTHER BOOKS AVAILABLE

Heaven, Can We get There?
Adam and Eve Cosmic Code
Rainbow Caper
Home Baking Business
Home Baking for Profit
Real Estate Math
June Bug
God Power
Finger Pirates
Love Affair in Occupied Japan
Architects Reference Manual
Journey to Terra Incognita
Child Discipline Vs. Spanking

www.ingramcontent.com/pod-product-compliance
Lightning Source LLC
Chambersburg PA
CBHW060241290526
45789CB00001B/140